I Hear Voices, and That's a GOOD Thing!

JAMES W. MOORE

I Hear Voices, and That's a GOOD Thing!

Abingdon Press
NASHVILLE

I HEAR VOICES,
AND THAT'S A GOOD THING!

This book is printed on acid-free paper.

Library of Congress Cataloging-in-Publication Data

Moore, James W. (James Wendell) 1938-
 I hear voices, and that's a good thing! / James W. Moore
  p. cm.
 ISBN 978-1-4267-4216-3 (pbk. : alk. paper) 1. Christian life—Methodist authors. 2. Christian life Biblical teaching. I. Title
 BV4501.3.M6628 2011
 248.4—dc23

                              2011034910

11 12 13 14 15 16 17 18 19 20—10 9 8 7 6 5 4 3 2 1
MANUFACTURED IN THE UNITED STATES OF AMERICA

In loving memory of

Mildred and Everett Daniels,

and

Jimmie Louise and Wendell Moore,

whose voices from heaven

we still hear

CONTENTS

INTRODUCTION

In the spring of 2010, country music singer Chris Young came out with a recording that quickly zipped up the country music charts all the way to number one. It was called "Voices" and, in the song, Young sings about how every day he hears voices from the past that help guide him through life, voices from the past that make him the person he is today, voices from the past that help him to make good choices and to know right from wrong. He sings about these valuable voices in his head—the voices of his parents and grandparents reverberating in his heart and mind, giving him words of wisdom to help him find his way. Toward the end of the song, as he reflects on these voices that are constantly and persistently running around in his brain, he sings these poignant words:

> But I thank God for 'em
> 'Cause they made me who I am.

The first time I heard that song on the radio (country music is big in Texas), I found myself resonating to it and identifying with it because I also have great appreciation for the "voices" in my head that help me, encourage me, teach me, inspire me, comfort me, challenge me, and guide me.

Like Chris Young, I am grateful for the voices of my parents, grandparents, teachers, pastors, and friends who over the years have shared with me helpful words of wisdom that are still relevant for the living out of these days, words of wisdom that help me better relate to life, to other people, and to God.

But as a Christian, I am also uniquely blessed and fortunate to hear some other amazing voices that persistently echo in my head and heart. As a Christian, I am constantly hearing voices from the great personalities of the Bible. Every day, these amazing voices from the Scripture reverberate in my mind. When faced with choices and decisions, when trying to sort out priorities, when my heart is sad or glad, when challenges and problems thrust themselves into my life, when I need a word of assurance, or when faced with a new opportunity, I hear the voice of Jesus, the voice of Mary, the voice of Abraham and Micah and Esther and the apostle Paul and many other biblical voices whispering (or shouting!) to me powerful words that shape and direct my life. And when I hear these incredible and helpful voices, I can say with Chris Young:

I thank God for 'em
'Cause they made me who I am.

That's what this book is about: the celebration of the voices from the Bible that undergird and strengthen us in so many helpful, productive, creative, and redemptive ways. So, the bottom line is this: "I hear voices, and that's a good thing!"

CHAPTER ONE

I Hear the Voice of Jesus Saying, "Let Your Light Shine"

SCRIPTURE: MATTHEW 5:13-16

R ecently I ran across a detailed plan on "How to Become a Public Speaker." Here is what you do: You fill your mouth with a bunch of marbles, and then you begin to speak. After the first day, you take out one marble and go on speaking. On the second day, you take out a second marble and continue speaking. On the third day, you take out a third marble, and so on, until all the marbles are gone. When you have lost all your marbles, you become a public speaker!

You may think I have lost all my marbles, because I want to think with you in this chapter about *saintliness*, about what it means to be a saint. Who on earth wants to be a saint these days, in this kind of world? The very word conjures up ideas of all sorts of unreal people, people who live in stained glass windows or on pages of Scripture, or people who at least have been dead for many years. Today we use the word *saint* occasionally to describe a pious person, but the kind we don't want to be, the kind we subtly denounce and quickly disassociate ourselves from by saying rather dramatically, "I'm no saint!"

Remember the man who said, "My wife may not be a saint, but she is an angel. She *must* be an angel, because she's always up in the air, she's always harping on my faults, and she never has an earthly thing to wear!" Or remember the little boy who was caught by his mother just as he was snatching cookies from the cookie jar. "Oh, Tommy, how could you?" asked his mother. "Only last night you prayed that you wanted to become a saint. Do you remember that?" "Yes," Tommy answered, "I remember, but I wanted it to be only after I was dead!"

We can all relate to Tommy can't we? It's okay to be a saint, but not *now*, not these days. We want to sow our wild oats first. We don't want to be pious stuffed shirts. That's the way we seem to feel about saintliness. Who in this world, this life, wants to be a saint?

Will Rogers saw it clearly, and he cut right to the heart of it. Commenting on his visit to Rome, he said he found it interesting that "everybody wants to see where Saint Peter was buried, but nobody wants to try to live like him." I guess we could all afford to think about that a bit, couldn't we?

Actually, the word *saint* is a good word gone wrong. The apostle Paul used it frequently and evidently gave it a completely different meaning. In fact, he didn't use the word *saint* to refer to pious, sanctimonious, puritanical people at all. If you study his letters in the New Testament closely, you will notice that he writes to the saints in Rome, Corinth, Ephesus, and Philippi, and that there was nothing unreal or pietistic about them. They were not dead, either, but very much alive— sometimes a little livelier than Paul wanted them to be.

Paul sometimes even called these people *saints* and then proceeded to scold them for unsaintly behavior! What are we to make of this? Are we called to be saints? Now? In this world? The answer is YES; the biblical answer is ABSOLUTELY; but, we have to reclaim the word, redefine it, re-understand it.

As the old saying goes, "You can call me anything, if you let me define the terms!" So, let me define the term and describe what I think a true, genuine *saint* is.

This is not a textbook answer, not a dictionary definition, but an understanding out of my own personal experiences with people who were saints to me in the best sense of the word. It has been my experience that a genuine saint is simply a person who makes goodness attractive, a person who has a radiant, attractive, contagious commitment to God.

We have mixed it all up and turned it all around. A true saint is not one who turns you off spiritually, but just the opposite: *one who makes goodness attractive.* A real saint is not one who is so pietistic or prudish or sanctimonious that you can't stand it, but rather one who makes goodness so attractive and so appealing that when you are with him or her, you find yourself challenged and feeling, *I wish I could be more like that.* Jesus is calling us to be this kind of saint in the text for this chapter: "Let your light shine before others, so that they may see your good works and give glory to your Father in heaven" (Matthew 5:16). Now, let me list some saintly qualities I have seen in other people whom I have found to be special, radiant, attractive, appealing, challenging, and winsome.

First, a Saint Is One Who Makes It Easy for Others to Believe in God

We have heard the saying many times, but it still rings true: The surest evidence of God is a committed Christian. The best argument for the faith is a person who really lives it, as the poet Edgar A. Guest observed when he wrote, "When I see a deed of kindness, / I am eager to be kind" (from "Sermons We See," *Collected Verse of Edgar A. Guest* [Chicago: Reilly and Lee], 1934).

A real saint makes goodness attractive. He makes it easy for others to believe in God.

Let me tell you about Dr. Van Bogard Dunn. With a name like that, you would have to be a saint or a fighter; he was a little bit of both. Bogard Dunn influenced my life greatly first as a pastor and later as the dean of the seminary I attended. He was so committed that when I was in his presence I found it easier to believe. He made goodness and faith challenging, exciting, and special.

While in seminary, I accompanied Dr. Dunn on some recruiting trips. We would visit colleges and tell them about our school. He would speak as the dean, and I would speak as a student. On one occasion, we visited a college in Birmingham, Alabama. When we arrived we were exhausted, having been on the road for three or four days. We had driven all night with no sleep. We talked with students and faculty members all day and into the night, our schedule so full that we had no time to eat. About 9:30 that night we finished up and headed for the hotel, hungry, physically tired, mentally and emotionally wrung out. To make matters worse, it was raining. All I had on my mind was food and sleep as we walked through the drizzle, down the sidewalk toward the hotel in downtown Birmingham.

As we walked along, I suddenly realized that I was alone. Dr. Dunn had disappeared. I turned around and saw him about fifteen yards back, kneeling on the sidewalk, talking to a little boy who was leaning against a light pole. The little boy, who looked to be about eight or nine years old, was crying. I had been so tired that I had walked right past the little guy, but Dr. Bogard Dunn had seen him and heard his crying, and he had stopped to find out what the trouble was.

The boy said, "My father sent me to the corner grocery to get some things. I have the list, but I lost the money. I'm afraid to go home because I know he will beat me." Dr. Dunn took the boy by the hand, and together the three of us walked to the corner store, where Dr. Dunn paid for the little boy's groceries. The boy took the sack of groceries and ran hurriedly down the street. Then suddenly he stopped, came back, and said to Dr. Dunn, "Mister, I don't know who you are, but I sure do wish you were my daddy."

After that, I forgot about being tired and hungry. I walked around Birmingham for two hours in the rain, trying to find somebody, anybody, I could help!

A true saint is not one who is nauseatingly pious, but rather a saint is one who inspires us and challenges us and brings out the very best in us. A real saint is radiant, making goodness attractive and making it easier for others to believe in God.

How powerfully we see this in Jesus—the power of his influence. Think of the lives he touched: because of him, the weak and vacillating Simon Peter became a rock; Mary Magdalene became, instead of a woman of the streets, a woman of faith; the self-seeking James was transformed into a self-giver who gave everything, even his life. It wasn't just what Jesus did; it was what others did because of him. It was the touch of his influence.

What about you? How about *your* influence? Do you make it easy for others to believe or do you make it hard? Paul Gilbert wrote "You are writing a Gospel, a chapter each day," in terms of our words and our actions. Gilbert goes on to point out that others are paying attention to us accordingly and are taking note of whether we are acting in faith ("Your Own Version," *Daily Guideposts*, October 13, 1990).

That's the first thing: A true saint is one who makes it easy for others to believe in God.

Second, a Saint Is One Who Believes the Best Things in the Worst Times

A saint remains faithful under pressure, is spiritually tenacious, keeps on believing when it is difficult.

Harry Emerson Fosdick underscored the importance of this special quality when he told a story that came out of the Armenian atrocities of the 1940s.

A young woman and her brother were chased into an alley by a Turkish soldier. Trapped, the sister watched as the soldier brutally murdered her brother. Horrified, scared, and heartbroken, she was able to scramble over the wall and escape for the moment. A few days later however, she was captured by the Turks, and since she was a nurse, she was forced to work in a military hospital.

One day, into her ward and under her care was brought the same Turkish soldier who had killed her brother. He was very ill. They recognized each other immediately. Fosdick writes that the slightest inattention to his care would have quickly brought on the soldier's death.

The young nurse told later of the bitter struggle that took place within her. One part of her cried, "Vengeance, he killed your brother; get even, this is your chance; it would be so easy, no one would ever know." But the voice of Jesus, the teachings of Jesus, teachings she had believed and practiced for many years, welled up in her soul: *Love; forgive; be merciful!* The voice of Jesus won the day, and she conscientiously nursed the soldier back to health. Later, the soldier, unable to restrain his curiosity, asked the young nurse, "Why? You recognized me, I know. Why didn't you let me die?" She answered, "I am a follower of him who said 'Love your enemies and do them good.'" The soldier was silent for a long time and then replied, "I never knew that there was such a religion. If that is your religion, tell me more about it, for I want it." (Harry Emerson Fosdick, *Twelve Tests of Character* [New York: Richard R. Smith, 1931], pages 166-67.)

A saint is one whose faith is radiant and appealing, one who keeps on believing even when it is difficult, one who believes the best things in the worst times.

Third, a Saint Is One Who Does Ordinary Things in Extraordinary Ways

What God really needs is not so much extraordinary people who do extraordinary things, but ordinary people like you and me who do ordinary things in extraordinary ways.

I was thinking recently of Pop Sandlin, who influenced my life greatly. He touched the lives of many young people. He was a youth counselor at my home church in Memphis. He couldn't have preached a sermon for anything, couldn't carry a tune in a bucket, couldn't teach a class, couldn't lead a public prayer, and couldn't teach a Sunday-school lesson. He was shy but he was genuine, and you knew it immediately. He loved God and the church, and he really cared for young people.

He made terrific hamburgers. Every Sunday night he was at the church cooking hamburgers and driving kids to and from the church. Pop Sandlin gave me a poem that I used in the first sermon I ever preached, and I have kept it in my files over the years. It's called "The Man with the Consecrated Car."

> He couldn't speak before a crowd;
> He couldn't teach a class,
> But when he came to Sunday School
> He brought the folks 'en masse'.
>
> He couldn't sing to save his life;
> In public couldn't pray;
> But always his 'jalopy' was
> Just crammed on each Lord's Day.
>
> And though he couldn't sing, nor teach,
> Nor even lead in prayer,
> He listened well; he had a smile,
> And he was always there—
>
> With all the others whom he brought
> Who lived near and far—
> And God's work was greatly prospered
> For he had a consecrated car.

I am convinced that the church is paralyzed not so much by the lack of people to do great things, but by the unwillingness of people to do the little things. What we need more than anything are some Pop Sandlins. We need people to do ordinary things in extraordinary ways.

Finally, a Saint Is One Who Loves Even the Unlovable

This was one of the crowning qualities of Jesus' life— to see and reach out and touch that person nobody else cared about or noticed.

Some years ago, I received a letter from a woman in East Texas who was a shut-in. She was writing to say that our televised church services were rays of sunshine in her rather dismal existence. She described what it is like to be a shut-in. I felt so sorry for her. It must be hard to be shut in, but it is even worse to be "shut out." Love means acceptance, inclusion, and belonging, and there is nothing more saintly than loving in this way— loving the outcast, loving the unlovable. Nothing is more Christlike than that.

In his book *The Miracle of Love* (Fleming H. Revell Company, 1971, page 82), Charles Allen tells the story about a little girl showing a man her dolls. She had lots of dolls of all shapes and sizes. "Tell me," said the man, "which one is your favorite doll?" The little girl hesitated for a moment and said, "You promise you won't laugh if I show you my favorite?" The man promised. The girl ran out of the room. In a moment she returned, and in her hands she held an old, dirty, tattered, dilapidated doll. Some of its hair had come off, its nose was broken, and its cheeks were scratched. An arm and a leg were missing. "Why do you like this doll best?" asked the man. The little girl replied, "I love her most because I'm afraid if I didn't love her, no one else would."

Who in the world wants to be a saint today? If it means being one who makes it easy for others to believe in God, if it means believing the best things in the worst times, if it means doing ordinary things in extraordinary ways, if it means loving even the unlovable, then that's my wish and hope and prayer for all of us—to hear the voice of Jesus flooding into our hearts and minds, saying, "Let your light shine before others, so that they may see your good works and give glory to your Father in heaven" (Matthew 5:16).

CHAPTER TWO

I Hear the Voice of Abraham Saying, "Let There Be No Strife Between You and Me"

SCRIPTURE: GENESIS 13:8-13

It happened in March of 1991. I was speaking at our church board meeting when someone handed me a note indicating that President George H. W. Bush would address the nation and the world at 8:00 P.M. on all the major television networks. So we quickly concluded our business session and went into an area of the church with a large-screen TV to hear the president speak.

He gave the news we had been waiting, hoping, and praying for over the last several weeks and months: THE WAR IS OVER! Combat action would be suspended at midnight that evening. Peace negotiations and the shut-down of the war effort were to begin immediately. In homes across the globe, in shopping malls, in sports arenas, on military bases, in churches, and out in the streets, in all nations, people stopped and listened and cheered.

Some cheered loudly and exuberantly, thrilled that the war was behind us. Others cheered quietly, more cautiously, hoping and praying that there would be no foul-up, or miscalculation or antagonistic reaction that would start up the hostilities again.

As I drove home from church that night I felt a sense of relief and my mind darted back over the last few days to numerous poignant pictures connected with this war in the Persian Gulf, powerful images that somehow had locked themselves dramatically into my head and heart. For example:

- the picture of President Bush soberly announcing the start of the ground war;
- the image of people coming daily to the altar of our church to pray for peace;
- the picture of a family in Detroit, Michigan, who had two sons fighting in the war but on opposite sides, one an American Marine, the other an Iraqi foot soldier;

- the image of yellow ribbons everywhere—on trees and doors and gates and lapels. I even saw a homeless man pushing a grocery shopping cart, which held all of his earthly possessions, and on the front of it was a big yellow ribbon;

- and who could ever forget the picture of thousands of Iraqi soldiers waving white flags and leaflets, eager for the chance to surrender, starved for food and water, some even surrendering to an Italian cameraman and others surrendering to reporters from major news organizations;

- the image of Iraqi prisoners of war grabbing desperately for food and telling of how they had lived for twenty-eight days on nothing but grass and rainwater;

- the picture of a young Kurdish soldier who said that he was forced to serve in the Iraqi army after his two brothers were killed because they had refused to volunteer;

- the picture of a Saudi Arabian soldier helping a weakened Iraqi soldier out of his bunker, and then seeing the Iraqi soldier smile and reach over to kiss the Saudi soldier in gratitude;

- the image of little children writing letters to First Lady Barbara Bush to express their support and their concerns, with one little girl telling Mrs. Bush that she had been praying for President Bush every night (and then, as a P.S., thanking Mrs. Bush for breaking her foot in a sledding accident, saying, "No other First Lady would have done that for us");

- the picture of General Norman Schwarzkopf giving that now famous press conference in Saudi Arabia, outlining the details of the war effort in his familiar, authoritative style and prompting the late radio commentator Paul Harvey to say, "When General Schwarzkopf says, 'Sit down!' you don't even look to see if there is a chair!"

- the painful image of 95 percent of the people in Baghdad drinking and bathing in the Tigris River, one of the most polluted rivers in the world;

- the somber picture of hundreds of blazing oil wells scorching the earth, and burned-out cars, tanks, and vans littering the roads and desert spaces;

- the picture of people by the thousands dancing in the streets of Kuwait City, hugging one another, celebrating their freedom, and thanking coalition soldiers and even reporters;

- and then there was the picture of Army Specialist Christine Mayes from Rochester Mills, Pennsylvania. She had gotten engaged to be married on February 17 and on that day left for Saudi Arabia.

Eight days later, a Scud missile slammed into her barracks on the outskirts of Dhahran. Twenty-nine American soldiers were killed, and ninety-nine more were injured. One of those who died was Christine Mayes. She had been engaged for eight days. She was twenty-two years old.

On and on I could go with a touching litany of these powerful freeze-frame pictures etched forever into so many hearts and minds. As I thought of these heart-wrenching events, I found my mind moving back further in time to something that happened thousands of years ago in that same Middle East region. This event happened not many miles from Kuwait, and it too revolved around a land dispute. We find the story recorded in the thirteenth chapter of Genesis.

Abraham (who was at that time called *Abram*), the father of the Jewish nation, and his nephew Lot, were having a problem. Their herdsmen were doing battle. Strife had arisen between them. They had not learned how to share the fruits of the land. They could not get along. Conflict, bickering, quarreling, fighting, and animosity were ruling the day. The herdsmen of Abraham and the herdsmen of Lot were at one another's throats in deciding how the land was to be divided and used.

Then Abraham stepped forward. Despite his seniority in age and rank and family position, Abraham chose to deal with the problem as a peacemaker. He said to Lot, "Let there be no strife between you and me. You choose first. If you take the left, then I will go to the right; or if you take the right, then I will go to the left. But let there be no strife between us" (Genesis 13:8-9, paraphrased).

Here we see the magnanimity of Abraham, the exquisite picture of grace and generosity, the image of a man who (in the spirit of the God he served) chose to be a humble reconciler, and he uttered those words that have resounded across the centuries, a mountain-peak moment in the Bible and one of my favorite verses of Scripture: "Let there be no strife between you and me" (Genesis 13:8).

Hundreds of years later, Jesus surely must have had this moment in mind when he spoke those powerful words in the Sermon on the Mount, words that still ring so true: "Blessed are the peacemakers, for they will be called the children of God" (Matthew 5:9). What does that mean? Simply this: There is nothing in this world more godly or more godlike than the ministry of reconciliation, than the work of peacemaking.

Abraham was a peacemaker, and if you read on in the story you will see that he received God's blessing. Lot's arrogance and selfishness and aggressiveness caused him all kinds of problems, but Abraham's peacemaking-ways served him well and brought joy to the heart of God.

"Let there be no strife between you and me"; what a great verse of Scripture that is! What a great spirit to live by and to live out. Let me show you what I mean.

Apply the Gracious Spirit of Abraham to the World Scene

If nation could say to nation, "Let there be no strife between you and me," that would surely make the heart of God glad. Marshall McLuhan called it the "global village" concept. Whatever we call it, it means the same thing: because of the incredible advances in travel and telecommunications, we now live in a rapidly shrinking world, a world where, with every passing day, we become more aware of one another and, in some ways, more interrelated with one another.

Walt Disney was right, "It's a small world after all," and the lesson is obvious: We in the world must stop seeing other nations as enemies and see them instead as neighbors with whom we share our global village and to whom we can say, "Let there be no strife between you and me." We in our world must declare a moratorium on hate.

James Armstrong, in his book *Gentlemen Start Your Engines*, reminded us of how irrational hatred is in international affairs. He said,

> Think of us here in America:
>
> In 1755 there was the French and Indian War. We were told to hate the French and love the British.
>
> In 1776, there was the American Revolution, and we were told to hate the British and love the French.
>
> In 1799, we were mad at the French again, and in 1812, we were at odds with the British again.
>
> In 1861, there was the Civil War, and the North and South hated each other.
>
> In one decade we love the Chinese and hate the Japanese . . . and then we love the Japanese and hate the Chinese. We just don't know about Russia. In Korea, we hated every one north of an imaginary line and in Vietnam things were even more confused. (Spiritual Life Publishers, 1967)

Now, I don't know how you feel about James Armstrong's observations, but I do know this: I was taught long ago in Sunday school not to hate anybody. When we stop seeing other nations as enemies to be hated and start seeing them as friends and neighbors to be loved in this global village of ours, then we can say to them, "Let there be no strife between you and me," and then we are on the way to peace.

Think of Abraham's Gracious Spirit as It Applies to Families

If family members could say to one another, "Let there be no strife between you and me," that too would make the heart of God glad.

That's what the story in Genesis 13 is about—a family squabble. Abraham solved it by taking the high road, by being a reconciler. He could have complained, he could have squabbled, he could have demanded his rights, but no! Abraham chose the way of grace and peace and said to his nephew, "This has gone on long enough. This is not good. Let's settle it! Let's make it right! Let there be no strife between you and me."

It never ceases to amaze me how torn apart families can get, and often over the silliest things. Some years ago, I visited with a family whose problem could have been solved in five minutes if their arrogant selfishness could have given way to just a little love and goodwill. Members of that family had not spoken to one another for months because of some ridiculous misunderstanding over who should inherit a clock that wouldn't even run. A broken clock not worth twenty-five dollars was ripping this family to shreds.

Listen! If there is a problem in your family, go fix it today. Swallow your pride and go make it right today. Don't let another minute pass. Life is too short for that kind of family estrangement. It's not worth it. It will make you sick physically and spiritually. For God's sake, for your sake, for your family's sake, go today and say it: "Let there be no strife between you and me."

Think of the Spirit of Abraham Theologically

You know where Abraham got that gracious spirit, don't you? He got it from God. He was imitating the generous, forgiving, reconciling spirit of God. Some years later that reconciling nature of God was seen more dramatically in the gift of Jesus Christ to this world. When God sent Jesus Christ into the world, he was saying to the world, to you and me, "Let there be no strife between us."

"For God so loved the world that he gave his only Son, so that everyone who believes in him may not perish but may have eternal life" (John 3:16). God so loved the world that he gave his only son to become our peace, the one who breaks down the dividing walls of hostility.

In the February 1991 edition of *Life* magazine, there was a powerful article entitled "Lee Atwater's Last Campaign" (pages 58–67), written by Lee Atwater with

Todd Brewster. Just one year earlier, Lee Atwater had been the chairman of the Republican National Committee. He was a rough and tough politician known widely as the "pitbull" of American politics. But then, Lee Atwater became a changed man. "I have found Jesus Christ," he said. "It's that simple. He's made the difference and I'm glad I found him while there's still time."

In March of 1990, Lee Atwater was making one of his hard-driving speeches. He had just made a cynical attack on Michael Dukakis, the 1988 Democratic candidate for President. Suddenly Atwater's left foot and leg and then his whole side began to shake and twitch uncontrollably. And then, he collapsed. Later, at the hospital, Lee Atwater and his family learned the cause: inoperable brain cancer. Life changed for Atwater. As a photo caption with the *Life* article indicates (page 67), he stopped reading Machiavelli and started reading the Bible. And God came into his life as never before.

In a separate interview, Atwater explained, "I have found Jesus Christ. It's that simple. . . . I don't hate anybody anymore. . . . For the first time in my life, I don't hate somebody. I have nothing but good feelings toward people. [There's] just no point in fighting and feuding" (Associated Press, "Atwater Tries to Make Peace with Former Political Foes," *New York Times*, November 3,

1990; www.nytimes.com/1990/11/03/us/atwater-tries-to-make-peace-with-former-political-foes.html [accessed August 11, 2011]).

Writing in the *Life* magazine article, Atwater said,

> I've come a long way since the day I told George [H. W.] Bush that his 'kinder, gentler' theme was a nice thought, but it wouldn't win us any votes. I used to say that the President might be kinder and gentler, but I wasn't going to be. How wrong I was. There is nothing more important in life than human beings, nothing sweeter than the human touch.

As the *Life* article indicates, Lee Atwater spent the rest of his days making peace with former enemies. He said "I'm sorry." He wrote letters of penitence asking for forgiveness. He said that God had given him a new lease on life, and he wanted to spend the rest of his time on this earth telling the world of God's redeeming, reconciling love.

That's the way it works. When God's reconciling love comes into us—really comes into us—it changes us, and then we want to imitate God's gracious, reconciling ways. Then the spirit of God's love flows through us and out to others. Then we want to take up the gracious voice of Abraham and say to everyone we meet, "Let there be no strife between you and me."

CHAPTER THREE

I Hear the Voice of Joseph Saying, "You Meant Evil Against Me, But God Meant It for Good"

SCRIPTURE: GENESIS 50:15-21

There's absolutely no getting around it: At one time or another, all of us have to face trouble. It is universal and impartial, and not one of us is immune. There is no wall that is high enough to shut out trouble. There is no life, no matter how much it may be sheltered, that can escape from it. There is no trick, however clever, by which we can evade it.

Sometime, somewhere, and maybe even when we least expect it, things will go wrong! Trouble will rear its head, thrust its way into our lives, and confront and challenge every single one of us.

The psalmist did not say, "I will *meet* no evil"; he said, "I will *fear* no evil"! (See Psalm 23.)

It can happen so quickly; so very quickly, things can go wrong! Remember how Frank Sinatra used to sing it in "That's Life": "Riding high in April, shot down in May." So quickly, life can cave in around us.

We see it graphically in the Joseph story in the Book of Genesis. One moment Joseph was the son of a well-to-do man, with bright hopes for a happy, secure, and prosperous future; the next moment, his world had caved in around him, and he had become a slave in a strange, foreign, and hostile land.

One thing that has made Joseph live so vividly in the minds of people over the years is the fact that his story is so true to life. We can relate to it. Of course, we don't get sold into slavery, but we all do have things go wrong for us. In school, in business, in marriage, in health, in our hopes for our children, in our personal relationships, things can go wrong, things do go wrong.

And when they do, we need to remember Joseph. Remember that Joseph was one of the twelve sons of Jacob. He was his father's "favorite son." Now, this favoritism, which Joseph enjoyed and flaunted, didn't set well with Joseph's brothers. They were jealous, envious, resentful, and bitter.

In fact, Joseph's brothers became so hostile toward him that they actually kidnapped him with the intent to murder him. But then, when some slave traders came by on their way to Egypt, Joseph's brothers sold him into slavery.

You may recall the rest of the story, how Joseph, through his faith in God and his unique ability to interpret dreams, eventually ends up governing Egypt, saving all of Egypt, as well as his own family, from famine. Joseph then sums it all up by saying to his brothers these powerful words: "You meant evil against me, but God turned it for good!" (Genesis 50:20, paraphrased).

The story of Joseph is a good one to remember when things go wrong because the story underscores four basic questions that often are raised when life caves in on us.

1. Whose fault is this?
2. How do we respond?
3. How can this situation be redeemed?
4. Where is God?

Let's look together at each one of these questions.

"Whose Fault Is This?"

Why did this happen? What caused it? Who is at fault here? Where can we lay the blame? This is quite often our first response when things go wrong. We look for someone to blame. Now, this ploy is as old as the garden of Eden. When things went wrong there, Adam pointed at Eve, and Eve pointed at the serpent.

We learn this tactic early in life. When our son was about six years old, he went through a period of "karate chopping" everything in sight. One day during this period, he ran through the kitchen and laid a karate chop on the dishwasher, accidentally hitting the *On* button. When the dishwasher started up, Jeff stopped dead in his tracks. He knew that he had done something he shouldn't have done. But quickly he rose to the occasion by saying, "It's OK, Dad—we'll tell mom *you* did it."

When things go wrong, isn't that what we often do? We ask, "Whose fault is this?" And we look for someone to blame it on.

In the Joseph story, there are several different ways you could answer the question of "whose fault is this." On the one hand, you could blame Joseph. Joseph was partly at fault, and partly he wasn't. He did fan the flames of his brothers' hostility with his swaggering bigheadedness (see Genesis 37:1-11). He was spoiled and childish. He did flaunt the fact that their father favored him. He did parade before them, tradition tells us, in his long-flowing coat of many colors (see Genesis 37:3). He did tell on his brothers when he saw them doing something they shouldn't have been doing. He did arrogantly reveal his two dreams, in which his eleven brothers fell down in worship before him. You could blame Joseph.

But still, on the other hand, this does not excuse his brothers for their harsh, cruel act of selling him into slavery and then deceiving their father, Jacob, into thinking that Joseph was dead (see Genesis 37:12-36). Surely they were at fault.

Then, too, it was father Jacob's fault also. If he had shown more sense in dealing equally with all his sons, Joseph probably never would have ended up as a slave in a foreign land.

But when you get right down to it, the truth is, it really doesn't matter who is at fault. The only real value derived from asking this kind of question is the hope that we can learn from our mistakes and grow from them and do better next time.

The problem here is that too often when things go wrong, we evade facing the reality of the problem by spending too much time, effort, and energy in laying the blame on someone . . . and that really doesn't help. It once was said about one fellow: "He met misfortune like a man . . . he blamed it on his wife!"

So when things go wrong, it is not nearly so important to find who is at fault as it is to find the right way to respond to the problem. That brings us to question number two.

"How Do We Respond?"

When things go wrong, we may or may not be responsible for the cause, but one thing is certain: We are responsible for the result, and the result depends on how we meet the situation, how we respond to trouble.

There are two possibilities here. We can respond with cowardice or with courage. We can respond with weakness or with strength. We can respond with bitterness or with "better-ness."

Picture Joseph riding along in that slave caravan going down into Egypt, scared, confused, bewildered, and panicky. How easy it would have been for him to choose the way of cowardice, to give in to self-pity, to quit on life. When things go wrong, many people do indeed choose that route. They blame God and die—maybe not physically, but emotionally, spiritually. They just give up, toss up their hands, throw in the towel, and wallow in self-pity.

But this was not so with Joseph. He grew up in that slave caravan. He had been a spoiled and selfish childish personality, but in that slave caravan he grew up and became a man. He chose the way of courage and trust in God. He didn't understand what was happening to him, but he kept on trying, kept on believing, and he trusted God to bring it out right. And God did!

When things go wrong, our calling as Christians is to choose life, doing the best we can, living one day at a time and trusting God to bring it out right.

Psychologists tell us that as long as we live, we have two desires working within us: first, we have the temptation to shrink back and quit on life, to give in to cowardice and bitterness and self-pity; and second, we feel the challenge to move forward through struggle and effort and courage and perseverance into a deeper dimension of life. And this, of course, is what Joseph did and what we, as people of faith, are called to do.

Now, when things go wrong, there is a third question.

How Can This Situation Be Redeemed?"

What could be a more Christian question for us than this one, we who have as the major symbol of our faith a cross! That's what the cross is:

- a situation redeemed
- a wrong turned right
- a bad thing turned into a good thing
- a defeat converted into a victory
- a death resurrected into a life

In other words, learn how to "suffer creatively." Writing about President Abraham Lincoln and the challenges Lincoln had faced, Harry Emerson Fosdick wrote,

> Quality of character never could have come from ease, comfort, and pleasantness alone. He did not simply endure his tragedies; he built character out of them. . . . trouble and grief can add a new dimension to life. No hardship, no hardihood; no fight, no fortitude; no suffering, no sympathy; no pain, no patience.
> . . . don't waste sorrow, it is too precious. . . . Don't misunderstand me. I'm not singing a hymn of praise to trouble. We all alike dread it, but it is inevitably here to be dealt with one way or another. . . . Some people end in defeat and collapse. . . . Others—thank God!—can say with Paul, "We triumph even in our troubles." (*Dear Mr. Brown: Letters to a Person Perplexed about Religion* [New York: Harper, 1961], pages 182-83)

Look at Joseph again. He had so many things go wrong: betrayed by his own brothers, sold into slavery, thrown into prison, the victim of a scorned woman (see

Genesis 39–40). What a hopeless situation! And yet it was there in prison that Joseph's ability to interpret dreams was made known to the ruler Pharaoh. It was there that a bad situation got redeemed. (See Genesis 41.)

Let me illustrate this further. Sometimes an oyster is invaded by a grain of sand. The sand irritates. The oyster tries to get rid of it. But when it cannot, it turns that same irritating grain of sand into a valuable pearl. *That's* redeeming the situation.

One of the stories about the well-known inventor Thomas Edison says that as a boy, he received a blow on one or both of his ears, which caused a hearing disability. Later, however, his hearing disability kept out distractions and enabled him to concentrate on his work, and the world has benefitted greatly from that.

There's a popular sermon illustration about George MacDonald, in one of his books, telling the story of a young woman in trouble who distressfully complains, "I wish I'd never been made." An older friend responds, "My dear, you are not fully made yet; you're only being made, and this is the Maker's process!"

I read recently of a man who was in an automobile accident. The doctor told him, "Both of your eyes are seriously injured. One eye can be saved, but the other eye will have to be removed and a glass eye put in. We need your consent." The injured man answered, "If you do have to put in a glass eye, could you please put one in that has a twinkle in it!"

When things go wrong, one of the best questions we can ask is: "How can this situation be redeemed?"

Now, there is one other question that is often asked when things go wrong, when our world caves in.

"Where Is God?"

Where is God? The answer, as Alfred Lord Tennyson put it, is that he is with you even "nearer than hands and feet," and as you keep moving forward, doing the best you can, trusting God, living one day at a time, God moves with you and brings you through the valley.

This is what Joseph meant at the end of his story when he said to his brothers, "You meant evil against me, but God turned it for good." He meant, "What happened was bad, but God was with me through it all, every step of the way, and in the miracle of his grace, he brought good out of these terrible events."

This is the good news of our faith. God is with us, and nothing, not even death, can separate us from him! Jesus said, "Lo I am with you always" (Matthew 28:20 KJV); this is God's most significant promise, and when you claim that promise, it will change your life.

Remember Dean Raimundo de Ovies's famous cemetery story. When he was a boy, he lived in England. He explained that the young boys back then had a habit of catching sparrows in the cemeteries at night. These sparrows would roost in the vines of the cemetery, and while they were asleep, they were easily caught.

One night he was in the cemetery catching sparrows, and he fell into a newly dug grave. The grave was so deep that he could not get out. He tried every way he knew, but to no avail. Finally, in exhaustion, he sat down in the corner of the grave to wait until morning.

But then he heard the footsteps of another boy, who had come into the graveyard looking for sparrows. The boy was whistling, as people are likely to do in grave-yards at night. Dean de Ovies recognized the boy as his friend Charlie. His first thought was to call out to Charlie for help, but he decided to wait for a while and see what would happen.

Sure enough, Charlie fell into the same grave. Dean de Ovies just sat quietly and unseen in the dark corner as Charlie tried frantically to get out. But nothing worked. Then, after a while, Dean de Ovies, in a deep voice, said loudly, "You can jump all you want to, Charlie, but you'll never get out of here!" But he did! In a single bound, Charlie went up and out of that grave as if he had wings!

There is a strong point here, namely, the power of motivation. If Charlie were that motivated by fear, why can't we turn the coin over and be that strongly motivated by confidence—the confidence that comes from claiming God's most significant promise, to always be with us. "Lo, I am with you always." When things go wrong, you can raise these questions, but more important, you can claim that promise! You can remember the confident and generous voice of Joseph saying, "You meant evil against me, but God turned it for good."

CHAPTER FOUR

I Hear the Voice of Moses Saying, "Do Not Be Afraid. . . . The Lord Will Fight for You. . . . Go Forward"

SCRIPTURE: EXODUS 14:10-15

Mark Twain once described the day he rushed to the top of Pike's Peak to see the sunrise. He said, "I got there on time but I missed it because I was looking the wrong way!" This is a common problem in life, isn't it? God has so many fantastic sunrises to show us, so many dramatic miracles to share with us, so many awesome wonders to reveal to us, but all too often we miss them because we are facing the wrong direction.

We have eyes, but so often we do not see; we have ears, but so often we do not hear; we have hearts, but so often we do not feel, because we are looking the wrong way, facing the wrong direction. Remember that powerful passage in the Book of Exodus where Moses experiences the presence of God in the burning bush. Moses is so moved by the sacredness of that moment, he "takes off his shoes" as an act of reverence—he is in fact standing on holy ground. (See Exodus 3:1-12.)

Reflecting on that burning bush episode, Elizabeth Barrett Browning wrote these words:

> Earth's crammed with heaven,
> And every common bush afire with God:
> But only he who sees takes off his shoes,
> The rest sit round it, and pluck blackberries.
> (from "Aurora Leigh"; 1856)

The way we see is so important, so crucial. Harold Kushner, in his book *Who Needs God?* expresses it like this:

> Religion is not primarily a set of beliefs, a collection of prayers, or a series of rituals. Religion is first and foremost a way of seeing. It can't change the facts about the world we live in, but it can change the way we see those facts, and that in itself can often make a real difference.
> (Fireside, 2002, page 21)

That is precisely what this remarkable story in Exodus 14 is about. It's about how people see things, how differently people may see the same situation.

On the one hand, look at what the people of Israel see here. They have just made camp at the Red Sea. They are filled with joy. This is a historic moment for them. This is their exodus, their deliverance, their salvation. After all those years of Egyptian slavery, now they are free. Moses is leading them out of bondage to freedom in the Promised Land.

But suddenly their beautiful dream becomes a ghastly nightmare. They turn around and look back, and on the horizon far off in the distance they see a huge cloud of dust, and they hear the unmistakable rumble of chariots. They know what this means: Pharaoh has changed his mind about releasing them. His army is coming after them. The people of Israel see themselves as doomed and done in. They see themselves trapped, pinned in, cornered, caught between the Pharaoh and the deep Red Sea. They are certain that they are going to be slaughtered in the desert. They see their situation as hopeless. You know why, don't you? It's because they are looking the wrong way.

But on the other hand, Moses sees it so differently. He turns his face toward God and sees an exciting, amazing, incredible new possibility. Notice, now, that Moses doesn't look to the past; he looks to the future! He doesn't look backward; he looks forward! He doesn't look at the strength of Pharaoh; he looks to the power of God! And because of what he sees, Moses is able to say with confidence to the people, "Fear not! Stand firm and see the salvation of the Lord, which he will work for you today. God will fight for you, so trust in him and go forward" (Exodus 14:13-14).

Now, *you* know the rest of the story. Moses and the people of Israel do indeed put their trust in God and go forward. God goes before them and opens the sea, leading them to safety and freedom on the other side. God comes to them in their hour of need. God saves them, protects them, delivers them. And listen—he can do that for you and me! That's the good news of the Bible and the strong message that explodes out of this story.

But the story here in Exodus 14 also confronts us with a crucial question, namely this: Are we looking the wrong way? Are we facing the wrong direction? Do we look at things with the eyes of fear or the eyes of faith? with the scared eyes of the Israelites or with the confident eyes of Moses? Let me bring this closer to home for us by breaking it down just a bit with three observations.

If We Can't See How to Believe, We May Be Looking the Wrong Way

That was the Israelites' problem that day at the Red Sea. They couldn't believe because they were looking the wrong way. They could see no hope because they were facing the wrong direction. God had to turn them around before they could see any way out of their predicament. That's the way it works. Before we can believe, the eyes of fear have to give way to the eyes of faith. We often hear the phrase "Seeing is believing," but actually it may well be more profoundly true the other way around: *Believing* is *seeing!*

This is precisely what happened to Francis of Assisi, and that change of vision is what made him a saint. He was awakened to a new way of looking at things, and that made all the difference. Francis was born into luxury, the son of a wealthy merchant. Early on, he had his eyes set on becoming a famous poet and a mighty warrior. He wanted fame and acclaim and power for himself. But during one of the military campaigns for his city-state, Francis of Assisi became ill, and he had to limp home in disgrace.

His adolescent vision of grandeur was reduced to shambles, and he went into a deep depression. He was so depressed that he retreated into a cave and remained there alone for almost two weeks. But there, in that cave, Francis was not really alone. God was with him, and God opened his eyes. God turned his life around. God saved him, delivered him, and gave him a new way of looking at things, and Francis of Assisi came out of that cave a new man who would go on to become one of the greatest servant-Christians in the history of the world. The name of Saint Francis is now synonymous with love and humility and service and self-giving.

We can see God everywhere we look if we have converted eyes, if we see with the eyes of faith. If we can't see how to believe, we may be looking the wrong way.

If We Can't See How to Forgive, We May Be Looking the Wrong Way

It's fascinating to watch how people act when trouble comes into their lives. You can tell a lot about a person by the way he or she handles a troublesome situation.

Sadly, all too often we think the first thing we have to do when trouble comes is to "find somebody to blame this on," and we can be so harsh, so unbending, and so unforgiving when we see it from that perspective.

That is precisely what the people of Israel did that day at the Red Sea. When they saw Pharaoh's army coming after them, they went into a panic, and they were quick to mouth and murmur, quick to gripe and complain, and quick to point the finger at Moses. "It's all your fault, Moses! Look what you have done to us! You should have left us alone! Our blood is on your hands! We will never forgive you for getting us into this mess!" You know why they reacted like that, don't you? It was because they were looking the wrong way.

A few years ago a minister friend of mine was conducting a funeral. He noticed a woman standing at the back of the sanctuary. The woman had arrived late and she stood, hugging the rear wall and crying throughout the memorial service. When the service ended, she came forward and in anguish hugged the casket. She broke down, sobbing and shouting into the casket, "I forgive you, Trudy! I forgive you! Can you hear me? Please hear me! I'm so sorry for the way I've acted. I love you. I forgive you. Please forgive me! Please forgive me!"

My minister friend went to her and put his arm around her shoulders and held her, trying to comfort her. He could feel her pain. She looked up at him through her tears, and she said, "My sister, Trudy, and I had a falling out some time ago. She begged me to forgive her. She tried everything to reconcile us. But over all these years I refused. I was so mean to her. I wanted her to pay for what she did to me. But I see now how wrong I was. I only wish to God I had listened to her. I loved her so much, and deep down I wanted things to be right with us, but now it's too late! I waited too long!"

Let me ask you something: Are you estranged from anyone like that today? *Are* you? Are you at odds with anybody? Are you cut off from someone? Are you hold-ing a grudge? Are you suffering the spiritual gangrene of a broken relationship? If so, go fix it! Go be recon-ciled! Go clear it up today, for their sake, for your sake, for God's sake. Go make peace!

Broken relationships are too painful, too stressful, too debilitating. They bring ulcers and headaches and in-somnia and loneliness. It's no way to live! Go fix it. Go in the spirit of Christ. Go in the spirit of forgiveness and be a peacemaker. But, you may say, "It's not my fault!" Well, it may not be your fault, but as a Christian, it is your responsibility. Jesus underscored that over and over again.

The teachings of Jesus make it abundantly clear that nothing pleases God more than to see us actively and tenderly loving one another and caring for one another, and nothing breaks God's heart more quickly than to see us being harsh and cold and hateful toward one an-other. If we can't see how to forgive, we are facing the wrong direction—we are looking the wrong way.

If We Can't See How to Trust, We May Be Looking the Wrong Way

That day when the Israelites felt trapped at the Red Sea, they lost their confidence. They were so blinded by the threat of Pharaoh's army that they failed to take into account the awesome power of God. Moses had to turn them around because they were facing the wrong direction. Moses had to remind them that God was with them, that God would fight for them, and that God would deliver them. Moses had to remind them to trust God and go forward. That's a message we need to hear, isn't it? Sometimes we simply have to trust God and go forward, and know with confidence that he will see us through and bring it out right.

Do you remember that scene from *The Sound of Music* where Maria is being sent out from the abbey to be the governess for Captain von Trapp's seven children? She's a little nervous as she walks down the road, but to rally her courage, she begins to sing "I Have Confidence." "Let them bring on all their problems . . . I'll make them see I have confidence in me," she sings. But just then Maria arrives and sees the huge, elegant, vast von Trapp estate, and she becomes intimidated, frightened, discombobulated. She stops singing, looks pleadingly toward heaven, and says prayerfully to God: "Oh help!" We can all relate to that, can't we? Sometimes life's problems simply overwhelm us, and all we can do is look to God and say, "Oh, God, help me!"

The good news is that we can always count on God to be there for us and to give us the strength we need. We can trust him. Dietrich Bonhoeffer put it like this:

"I believe that God will give us all the strength we need to help us to resist in times of distress. But he never gives it in advance, lest we should rely on ourselves and not on him alone" (Dietrich Bonhoeffer, *Letters and Papers from Prison*, Touchstone, 1997). And the hymn writer reminded us that if you will simply "Turn your eyes upon Jesus," then all of our earthly concerns will pale in comparison "in the light of his glory and grace" (Helen H. Lemmel, "Turn Your Eyes upon Jesus," 1922).

If we are listening, we can hear the voice of Moses saying, "Do not be afraid. . . . Trust God. . . . God will fight for you. . . . Go forward!"

CHAPTER FIVE

I Hear the Voice of King Saul Saying, "Remember to Put God First"

SCRIPTURE: 1 SAMUEL 31:1-7

The death of the successful young comedian Freddie Prinze in 1977, by a self-inflicted gunshot wound, was both tragic and haunting. It was such a quick end to such a quick and bright career. He seemed to have everything going for him. He had just been nominated for a Golden Globe award for his role in the popular TV series *Chico and the Man*; he had just signed a multiyear one-million-dollar contract with Caesars Palace in Las Vegas; he was negotiating film opportunities with two major studios; he had just been the guest host on *The Tonight Show*; and he had just performed for the president at one of the nationally televised inaugural events in Washington.

He was a bright, handsome, respected performer with an infectious smile and a brilliant career before him. He seemed to be on top of the world. Yet something was terribly wrong. Suddenly, there were drug problems, confusing business entanglements, the breakup of his marriage, and long periods of despondency. Then, at the age of twenty-two, in deep depression, he took his own life. He left a note saying the pressures were too great and he just could not go on any longer.

Now, please don't misunderstand me. It is not our place or purpose to judge Freddie Prinze, but somehow his experience seems to me to be a dramatic illustration of a basic, poignant truth of life, namely, that success can be dangerous.

Our own success can do us in. Prosperity has some treacherous pitfalls, and sometimes even while we seem to be winning, we may be losing something more valuable. What about you? Have you ever felt that you couldn't win for losing?

I heard about a man who tried to make it big in the stock market. He invested half his money in paper towels, and the other half in revolving doors. Then he said he got "wiped out" before he could "turn around"!

Sometimes you can't win for losing, and sometimes even while winning, you lose.

After the assassination of President John F. Kennedy, one of our theologians suggested that Americans know how to handle success and prosperity but are completely bewildered by adversity. Now we know what that theologian was talking about, but you know, I'm not so sure that his statement is completely accurate.

While it is true that most people, including us Americans, have trouble coping with hard times, it is still not quite true to say that we are totally adjusted to success. Recently, I was asked to speak to a group of business executives. The man who invited me told me that my listeners would be prosperous people who are trying to cope with the problems of success. They are over-committed, harassed by too many obligations, and feel guilty over the kind of lives they feel forced to lead. Many of them wonder if the compensations involved are worth the price they are paying. Of course, it was a generalization, but what he said does suggest the predicament of many people today.

Really, it is not a new problem. It is as old as the Bible itself, for even there we find people who could not win for losing, people who were upended by their own worldly success.

Take King Saul in the Old Testament, for example. He was the first king of Israel and one of the most tragic figures in history. He began his career as a shepherd boy caring for his father's flocks. His innate ability and the circumstances of the times conspired to catapult him to fame. He became king. He started out so well as the powerful, tall, handsome, courageous, charismatic young king who united his people and laid the foundation for Israel's later strength. But the mounting pressures and responsibilities of being king slowly got to him, and they undermined his personality. He became moody and suspicious and grew insanely jealous of young David's popularity, and then King Saul's life ended in catastrophe.

In the final act of his unhappy career (in a losing battle at Mount Gilboa), Saul drew his sword and fell upon it, ending his own life. Among his final words were these: "God has turned away from me and answers me no more" (1 Samuel 28:15). Now, what Saul meant by those words, we can't know for sure. I really think that it was not that God had left him, but that somehow Saul had drifted away from God. There was an emptiness, a vacuum in his life because somewhere along the way Saul lost something he meant to keep.

In a backdoor sort of way, we can learn much from the experience of Saul. We see in his tragic story the dangers of success. Let's take a look at some of them. Here are some I have listed, and I'm sure you will think of others.

There Is the Danger of Losing Our Priorities, Our Real Objectives, Our Sense of Purpose

You see, we can get so caught up in trying to succeed at all costs that we can forget what is really important, what really matters. I recently heard a basketball coach talking about his team. They were having a difficult season. They had lost several games in the last few minutes after having been far ahead. The coach said, "We can't stand prosperity. Every time we get ahead, we lose our concentration! We forget our game plan. We lose our sense of direction and start to drift. We forget what we are about, and before we realize what is happening, we have lost the game."

That's a pretty good parable for life, isn't it? The dangers of success; we can be defeated by our own successes if they cause us to lose our objectives, our purpose, our sense of what is really important in life.

I read the other day that a new commission has been appointed in our country to study and revise or remove laws that have become obsolete in some of our states. They have found some strange laws. In Hawaii, for example, it was illegal to put pennies in your ears; in

Wyoming, it was against the law to photograph rabbits between the months of January and April. One of the most interesting laws comes from the early days of the automobile. It reads, "When two automobiles arrive at an intersection at the same time, neither car shall move until the other car is out of sight." Obviously that law is impossible, but it makes an interesting point, namely that when two actions completely contradict each other, the result is a confusing paralysis.

This is precisely what happened to King Saul. He was paralyzed by two conflicting objectives. On the one hand, he wanted to be a wise, benevolent ruler and man of God; but at the same time he tried to feather his own nest and build an empire of personal power. No king ever governed more wisely than Saul in the early years of his reign. But in later years his objectives became confused. Dazzled by the possibilities of fame and fortune, he forgot his early goals, and this was his downfall.

Now, Saul's life should be a reminder to us all that fame and fortune are never valid goals in and of themselves. The only worldly success that gives us lasting satisfaction is that which comes as serendipity, as a by-product of service given to make this world a better place. As Jesus put it, "What do you benefit if you gain the whole world but lose your own soul?" (Mark 8:36

NLT). If Saul were here today, I think he would say to us, "Don't lose your objectives. Don't lose your purpose. Remember to put God first."

There Is the Danger of Resenting the Successes of Others

When King Saul began to resent the growing popularity of young David, his world began to crumble. Remember at first how he loved David. David was his court troubadour, his music-maker. David played his harp and he sang for the people, and everybody loved it. And Saul did too, until one day the people began to talk about how David was a better warrior than Saul. When Saul heard this, he couldn't stand it. He was so upset that he picked up a spear and threw it at David. (See 1 Samuel 18:1-16.)

Now, we have come a long way since then. We don't throw spears at one another. Or do we? Maybe we have our own modern-day ways of throwing spears of resentment, envy, or jealousy at one another.

There's an old story about a Methodist preacher who stood up at the annual conference meeting to give a report, and he had had a terrible year. Everything had gone wrong. The roof was leaking in his church, the walls needed painting, the heating bill was unpaid, there had been a drop in membership, the Sunday school attendance was falling off, and everything was in a terrible plight. "But," he said, "I have one point of good news, and that is that the Baptists aren't doing any better!"

How easy it is to give in to the sin of resentment of others. Believe me, there is nothing that will devastate your spiritual life more quickly than resentment. If Saul were here today, he would say to us, "Watch out for resentment! Don't give in to it. It will ruin your life."

There Is the Danger of Losing Your Family

The pressures of trying to succeed caused Saul all kinds of problems with his family. It still happens today. Have you heard the story about the little boy who said to his mother one evening, "Mom, when I die, will I go to heaven?"

"That's what the Bible teaches, Son," replied his mother. Then came another question: "Mom, when *you* die, will *you* go to heaven?"

"Yes, Son," she answered. The boy was silent for a moment, and then he said, "It's too bad Daddy can't go too, isn't it?"

"What in the world do you mean?" his mother asked. The little boy answered, "He'll be too busy working to go."

If Saul were here today I think he would say to us, "Don't neglect your families! There is no success or fame or fortune worth losing your family."

There Is the Danger of Forgetting Our Dependence upon God and upon Other People

This was Saul's problem most of all. Intoxicated by his own success and overconfident in his own wisdom and strength, Saul drifted away from God and from his closest friends. He began to think of himself too highly and to take himself too seriously. Our forefathers had a quaint but descriptive phrase. They said, "A fellow can get above his raisin'!" What they meant, of course, was that on the pinnacles of prosperity, it's so easy to forget our indebtedness to those who made it all possible. If we are not careful, we can lose our sense of gratitude to God and to others.

When Jenkin Lloyd Jones became editor of the *Tulsa Tribune,* he had risen from a buck-private reporter to the high position of editor in just eight years. Once, while teaching a group of students in journalism, one of the students asked Jones how he was able to move up to become editor so rapidly. Jenkin Lloyd Jones answered, "I owe it all to superior diligence, considerable natural ability, and a father who owned the newspaper."

Now, all of us are indebted to our heavenly Father, God, like that. You see, genuine success has nothing to do with money or fame or fortune or position or even accomplishments. I think if Saul were here today, he would say to us that the only real success, the only success that matters, is that sense of inner peace that comes from being "at one" with God and with his children.

It's not so much how the world feels about you but how you feel about yourself that counts, how you feel inside. To believe in yourself; to be able to love other people; to have a cause, a sense of mission and purpose; to feel that you are doing something with integrity to make this world better because you passed through it; to feel a sense of partnership with God in what you are and what you do—that's what winning is, that's what makes you feel good to be alive, that's richness beyond counting.

There is an old story of a sixteenth-century British sailor who sailed with Sir Frances Drake. When the sailor came home, people ridiculed him: "You don't have much to show for all those years, do you?" The old sailor replied, "No, I haven't much. I've been cold, hungry, desperately frightened—even shipwrecked. But I'm sure of one thing: I've been with the greatest captain who ever sailed the seas."

You see, God doesn't promise us prosperity or earthly riches or success. All he promises us is his love, his grace, his caring presence, and the riches of Christ, and that's the most important and valuable thing of all.

If you and I will listen closely, we can hear the voice of King Saul whispering in our ears these poignant words: "Don't lose your way! Don't be defeated by your own successes. Don't forget your priorities. Don't lose your purpose. Remember to put God first!"

CHAPTER SIX

I Hear the Voice of Esther Saying, "Don't Miss Your Moment"

SCRIPTURE: ESTHER 4:1-17

In the hit Broadway musical "Stop the World—I Want to Get Off," actor Anthony Newley played a kind of everyman character named Littlechap, and he sang a powerful song by the title of "Once in a Lifetime," which had a dramatic melody and these poignant words of destiny, calling and seizing the opportunity: "This is my moment. . . . I'm gonna do great things."

"This is my moment!" We have all known that feeling, haven't we? We have all known that special occasion when something stirs within us and we know that a unique opportunity is now available to us—maybe never to return again in just this way. We know the feeling of that crucial moment.

Sadly, however, we also must confess that we know the empty feeling of "missing our moment," of letting the moment pass. Because of fear or timidity or insecurity or procrastination, we let the moment slip through our fingers. We do nothing. We miss our moment, and then we deeply regret it because we know deep down that we cannot replace it; that special moment is gone forever.

How many letters have never been written?
How many phone calls have never been made?
How many compliments have been left unsaid?
How many *I'm sorry*'s remain unspoken?
How many *Thank you*'s have never been voiced?
How many *I love you*'s are still unexpressed?
How many commitments are still not made?
And all because we missed our moment!

If we put it off, the moment passes; the feeling subsides and is never expressed. And sadly, these missed moments can lead to heartache, disappointment, regret, and even tragedy.

Let me share with you three thoughts about this.

We See This "Missed-Moment Syndrome" Vividly in the Scriptures

The truth is that most of the tragic characters in the New Testament were simply people who missed their moment. Think of it.

- The Rich Young Ruler (see Matthew 19:16-22): He sees that the answer to his emptiness is in Jesus, but when Jesus calls him to follow, the young man turns away! He misses his moment.
- The Elder Brother (see Luke 15:25-32): He missed the party, the big celebration. His pride and resentment of his younger brother made him miss his moment.
- The One-Talent Servant (see Matthew 25:14-30): He squandered his opportunity and missed it.
- The Priest and the Levite (see Luke 10:25-37): They tiptoed by on the other side of the road to avoid someone in great need and missed their moment.
- The Ten Bridesmaids (see Matthew 25:1-13): They missed the wedding reception because they weren't prepared to respond at the right moment.
- Pontius Pilate (see Matthew 27:1-2, 11-24): Pilate held in his hands the life of Jesus. He could have

done great things. He could have said, "I was born for just such a time as this," but no, he washed his hands of the situation and he missed his moment.

- And what about Judas (see Matthew 26:47-56; 27:3-10)? He walked with Jesus, talked with him, ate with him, heard him teach, saw him do miraculous things, felt his love. Yet the tragedy of Judas's life is that he missed his moment.

The point is clear: The tragic people in history and in the Bible are those who missed their unique moments. The great people in history and in the Bible are those who seized their moment and acted with faith and courage.

This was illustrated by Leonard Sweet when he wrote "I Don't Do . . . ":

> The world's a better place because a German monk named Martin Luther did not say, "I don't do doors."
> The world is a better place because an Oxford don named John Wesley didn't say, "I don't do preaching in fields."
> (*Leadership*, Spring 1994, page 32)

Along those same lines, we can reflect upon Esther's actions and add these:

The World's a Better Place Because . . .
Esther didn't say, "I don't want to get involved."
Esther didn't say, "I can't take a chance; it's too risky."
Esther didn't say, "Who me?"

No, Esther seized the moment, and thousands of lives were saved.

Remember the Story of Esther with Me

Esther was exiled with her people in a foreign land, but amazingly she had caught the eye and the heart of the foreign king, Ahasuerus, and the king had made Esther his queen. The king was a powerful man. He ruled over 127 provinces from India to Ethiopia. The people of his kingdom looked up to him, but they also feared his power.

In fact, there was a law decreeing that no one could approach the king unless he called for them. To approach the king inappropriately was punishable by death, and yet, that is what Esther had to do. She had to approach the king in order to save her people.

The story is very much like an operetta with a powerful king, a beautiful queen, and now, entering stage left, is the villain. His name is Haman. Haman has been placed in charge of all the king's officials, and he gets caught up in his new power and commands that everyone has to bow down to him.

But Esther's cousin Mordecai (who was really like a father to Esther) refuses to bow down to Haman. Mordecai is devout in his Jewish faith, and he will not violate the Ten Commandments; he will not bow down to anyone but God. Haman is furious, and in his rage he devises a plan to kill off all the Jews throughout the kingdom.

Mordecai tells Esther about Haman's evil plan, and he tells Esther that she is the one who can stop this and save her people. He tells her that this is her moment, this is her destiny, this is her calling, that she has been placed in this position for just such a time as this.

Remember the Courage of Esther

Esther realizes that approaching the king is dangerous business; it could get her killed. But she says, "If I perish, I perish" (Esther 4:16), but somebody has to do something. Somebody has to take a stand. Somebody has to stop this killing. This is my moment. Come what may, I must do this. Esther courageously takes her stand, and through her act of bravery, she saves her people and thus becomes one of the respected and beloved heroes of the Bible.

What a great story this is, the story of Esther! And once again we see it: When we do our best, God will do the rest. He did it with Esther, and he can do it with you and me.

Esther seized the moment and saved the day, and her voice still resounds across the centuries, saying to us today, "Don't miss your moment! You may well have been born for just such a time as this!"

CHAPTER SEVEN

I Hear the Voice of Daniel Saying, "Read the Handwriting on the Wall and Tell It Like It Is"

SCRIPTURE: DANIEL 5:1-30

A new approach to sportscasting exploded on the American scene a few decades ago. The theme or slogan of this new way of describing a sporting event was "tell it like it is." The leading advocate of this tell-it-like-it-is approach was a brash, loquacious New York lawyer named Howard Cosell. Over the years, the late Howard Cosell may have become, because of his caustic style, "the man America loves to hate," but at the same time he influenced sportscasting in a way that changed the profession forever. Before Cosell, sportscasters tended to describe every ballgame as if it were the ultimate contest in the universe and every play as nothing short of miraculous. They covered over the mistakes and errors of players and coaches and made every player out to look like an All-American. But then along came Howard Cosell with his tell-it-like-it-is philosophy, demanding in his own controversial style that we all "tell it like it is," and this philosophy has touched not only the world of sports but also all of society.

If you stop to think about it, the call to "tell it like it is" implies something: it implies that we often don't! It suggests that much of the time we overlook how things really are or fail to see how it is or are unable to understand how it is or somehow that we are not bold enough to say how it is.

This is nothing new. This inability to see and perceive and understand "the handwriting on the wall" has been around for a long, long time. In fact, there is a story in the Old Testament, in the Book of Daniel, that shows this. A quick look at that story might help us understand better why people have trouble telling it like it is.

It's the story in Daniel of "the handwriting on the wall." In this story, the Jewish people are in captivity to the Babylonians. The Babylonian king, Nebuchadnezzar, has died and has been succeeded by his son Belshazzar. Belshazzar calls for a great feast for a thousand people. It was probably a state banquet, a very extravagant affair. At the banquet Belshazzar begins to show off, drinking in a blatant way before all the people. When he began to feel the effects of the wine, perhaps a bit tipsy and wanting to flaunt his power, he decides to make a show of strength. Arrogantly, he commands that the vessels of gold and silver that had been taken out of the Temple in Jerusalem be brought in, so that his lords and his wives and his concubines might drink wine from these sacred vessels. Not only do they drink from these cups and chalices, which were so holy to the people of the Jewish faith, they also use them to make toasts to some local deities, to idols, to the gods of gold, silver, bronze, iron, wood, and stone.

This was a terrible desecration of something holy, an awful display of disrespect. This was profaning the sacred, taunting the Jews and their faith. This was using the vessels of the Temple in drunken debauchery. But then, mysteriously, the large ghostlike fingers of a man's hand appear and begin to write on the wall of the palace these four words: "MENE, MENE, TEKEL, and PARSIN" (Daniel 5:25).

When Belshazzar sees the handwriting on the wall, he is terrified. He realizes he has gone too far. He turns white, he thinks deep thoughts, his body quakes, and his knees knock. He calls for his astrologers, his wise men, his advisors, his soothsayers. He wants somebody, *anybody*, to reassure him. He wants someone to say, "Don't worry about it. It's all right. There's nothing to fear; there's nothing significant here." But no such reassurance is forthcoming. Belshazzar's party has now become a nightmare. Terrified, he promises great rewards and power and position for anyone who can interpret the handwriting on the wall. But none of them can read it, and none of them can tell it like it is.

Belshazzar becomes all the more alarmed. His fear is contagious, sweeping across the banquet hall, and the noise of a frightened confusion erupts in the room. Down the hall, the queen mother hears the chaos. She comes in and reminds Belshazzar of Daniel, of Daniel's unique relationship with his God and his remarkable ability to explain riddles and solve problems and interpret dreams. So Daniel is called in. He sees "the handwriting on the wall," understands it, and then tells it like it is.

He says, "Oh, Belshazzar, you have made a big mistake! King Nebuchadnezzar, who served before you, was guilty of pride and idolatry; and now you, Belshazzar, have done the same and even worse. You have not humbled your heart, but you have lifted yourself up against the Lord of heaven. You have desecrated the sacred vessels of the temple. You have praised the gods of silver and gold and wood and stone, which do not see or hear or know. But the God who made you, the God who gave you breath, the God of destiny, you have not honored—thus the handwriting on the wall. Mene means your days are numbered; Tekel means you have been weighed in the balance and found wanting; Peres [the singular of Parsin] means your kingdom will fall and be divided" (Daniel 5:18-28, paraphrased).

The story ends by telling us that Daniel was right. That very night, Belshazzar was killed and his kingdom fell. With that dramatic Old Testament story serving as a backdrop, think about this: Of all those people, why was Daniel the only one who was able to understand and interpret the handwriting on the wall and "tell it like it is"? Think with me of the possibilities.

Some Were So Preoccupied That They Didn't See the Handwriting at All

They were so preoccupied that they missed the whole thing! After all, this was a big party, lots of spirits, lots of carousing. There were all kinds of distractions. It may well be that some had passed out from the wine, while others may have slipped out for even more festivities. That sounds pretty relevant for our times, doesn't it? Some are so caught up in the sights and sounds and distractions of partying that they miss the signs of the time, they miss the handwriting on the wall, and they miss the messages that come from the hand of God.

One of my favorite stories is the one about the young man in Paris, France, who came one day to see a psychiatrist. The young man was handsome and obviously wealthy. He said to the psychiatrist, "Please, help me. I feel so empty inside, so distressed, so unfulfilled. My life is going nowhere. I feel no sense of direction, no meaning, no purpose. I am bored, depressed, and unhappy. Please, help me!" The psychiatrist, who was an older man, looked at this young man with a twinge of envy, and he remembered Grimaldi. Grimaldi was the most notorious playboy in Paris. He was the most admired leader in France. The psychiatrist said to the young man, "I have the answer. I know how to bring you happiness: Go to Grimaldi. He will teach you how to enjoy life. Go to Grimaldi, and he will show you how to taste the pleasures of life. He will introduce you to the joys of living. He will show you how to be happy! He will show you how to have a full, vibrant life. Yes, that's the answer," said the psychiatrist. "Go to Grimaldi!"

"But, sir," said the sad young man, "I am Grimaldi!"

It has always been true that some people, in their frantic pursuit of pleasure and happiness, are blinded to the real truths of life. They chase after pleasure and miss purpose. They chase after mirth and miss meaning. They chase after all kinds of distractions and lose their direction. They are looking for love and life in all the wrong places and thus are missing God's handwriting on the wall. They can't tell it like it is because they are so distracted that they don't even see it.

Some See God's Handwriting on the Wall but Simply Don't Understand It

They don't know God's language. They see the words, but they can't read them. They see the signs, but they can't understand them. They see something happen but don't have the faintest idea what it means.

We see this in the way some people experience the Bible. For the most part, they ignore it. They spend no time with it. They don't study it; they know nothing of its contents. But then, in a moment of desperation, they grab up the Bible expecting some simple miraculous solutions to their problem, only to come up empty because they don't know the words, they don't understand the phrases, they don't know the themes, they don't know how to use the Bible, and they don't know how to find its treasures. We can't master the Bible in a few feeble attempts. We can only feel at home with the Bible and uncover its riches for us only after long exposure to its contents—after studying it and discussing it and meditating upon it and dialoguing about it.

Some saw the handwriting on the wall, but the words were strange and meaningless to them. They saw the handwriting on the wall, but they simply didn't understand it.

Some Didn't Think They Would Get a Hearing

Long ago, these members of the group had quit on life; they had thrown in the towel. "What's the use? The king doesn't listen to me anymore; he won't pay any attention to what I say. I'm a nobody." So, disillusioned, they just quit trying.

Some Didn't Have the Courage to Tell It Like It Is

"Telling it like it is" is not always fun. Being prophetic is risky, it's dangerous. It's not fun to tell "bad news" to a king. You could lose your head! In fact, in ancient times this often did happen. Kings, enraged by bad news, in anger and frustration sometimes would kill the messenger. Now, we have our ways—our discreet, contemporary ways—of "killing the messenger." When someone rises up and says something that judges us or indicts us or exposes us or makes us feel uncomfortable, we don't like that, and we want to silence that messenger. This is precisely what happened to Jesus. He "told it like it was," and they tried to silence him by nailing him to a cross. It's highly possible that some in King Belshazzar's banquet room that night saw the handwriting on the wall, and understood it, but just didn't have the courage to tell it or explain it.

Look at Daniel

Daniel is God's man of the hour. The queen tells the king of Daniel: "There is in your kingdom a man in whom is the spirit of the holy God" (Daniel 5:11, adapted). I wonder if anybody, anywhere, at any time, has ever said something like that about you or about me: "There is one in whom there is the spirit of the holy God." I wonder if anybody has ever sensed the presence of God in our lives like that. They sensed it in Daniel, and Daniel came and saw the handwriting on the wall. He understood what it all meant, and he had the courage to speak up and tell it like it is!

This is the calling of faith. This is the mission of the church—to see the word of God and to faithfully tell it, to see the message that we need a Savior and to help people accept and celebrate the glorious good news of the Christian faith: that a Savior is given to us, that a Savior is available. Lawrence Tribble put it like this:

One man awake, awakens another,
The second awakens his next-door brother.
The three awake can rouse a town,
By turning the whole place upside down.

The many awake can make such a fuss,
It finally awakens the rest of us.
One man up with dawn in his eyes,
Surely then multiplies.
(Lawrence Tribble, "Awake," ca. late 18th century)

Today, remember the strong voice of Daniel as he says to us, "Read the handwriting on the wall and tell it like it is!"

CHAPTER EIGHT

I Hear the Voice of Micah Saying, "Do Justice, Love Kindness, and Walk Humbly with Your God"

SCRIPTURE: MICAH 6:8

I don't want to be overly dramatic or overly emotional, and I certainly don't want to be partisan, but I would like to be very personal and very candid because I want to think with you about "the demoralizing of America." That phrase, "the demoralizing of America," has a double meaning. It means that we as a nation—that is, the United States of America—are in danger of losing our morals and our morale, in danger of losing our virtue and our spirit, in danger of losing our goodness and our soul.

I once read about a woman who phoned her TV serviceman and complained that something was wrong with her television set. The serviceman asked if there were any visible signs or symptoms. "Well, the newscast is on right now," said the woman, "and the reporter has a very long face." The serviceman replied, "Look, lady, if you had to report what's happening these days, you'd have a long face *too!*"

Indeed so. No matter what your political affiliation or stance may be, recent news reports, at just about any given time, can be demoralizing for all of us. Ongoing investigations, incessant accusations, military conflicts, the shaky stock market, and the menace of global terrorism both at home and abroad—all these things do indeed sap our spirits and give us heavy hearts and long faces. The truth is that there are some people in our country today who look at what's been happening in our nation in recent years, and they feel like things have turned upside down, that we are plunging down a steep and dangerous road with no steering wheel.

Now, let me hurry to tell you that I am an optimist by nature and by faith. I am an optimist about our country, and I strongly believe that we are going to come out of this. I love America! I love the dream of freedom in our nation. I love it that we are "the land of opportunity." I love our spiritual roots, our heritage, and our mission. And I genuinely believe that the

United States of America is the greatest nation to ever grace the face of this earth. I wouldn't want to live anywhere else. So, I'm not one of those pessimists or cynics who believe that we have lost the steering wheel. I do, however, see some treacherous bumps in the road. They are too glaring to miss! I do see some dangerous potholes that can indeed throw us out of control if we don't soon learn how to grab hold of that steering wheel again and get safely past them and back on the right track.

Let me mention three of these dangers that in my opinion are contributing greatly and dramatically to the demoralizing of America. Let me also put a footnote here: It is not my intention to place the blame on any particular political party or on any particular administration or any particular political leader. It is my intention to remind us that we are a family as the American people. We are all in this together, and it is high time for us in the American family to unite and stand tall and address these three dangers creatively and redemptively. It is not too late. In all three instances, the pendulum (over the years) has swung too far, and we need to swing it back! So, let's look together at the three dangers that are demoralizing America. Are you ready? Here is danger number one.

We Are in Danger of Losing Touch with Goodness

In our efforts to be tolerant (which is commendable), we have let the pendulum swing too far and consequently find ourselves in peril of forgetting the moral absolutes, the spiritual laws of the universe, the things that make America great: morality, virtue, integrity, truth, compassion, goodness. We seem to be in a moral quandary as a nation. We don't seem to know what goodness is anymore. Some blame it on the breakdown of the traditional family. Others blame it on the Supreme Court. Still others blame it on the church or on the entertainment world or on what has been called in recent years the "epidemic of me-ism."

One of the sad consequences of our moral drifting is that we have not connected our young people to the strong faith heritage of America. We have not taught them how deeply rooted in biblical faith was the birth of our nation! This was demonstrated some time ago by Jay Leno. He was doing his "Jaywalking" interviews one night. He asked some college students a few questions about the Bible. "Can you name one of the Ten Commandments?" he asked. One student replied, "freedom of speech?" Then Leno said to another college student, "Complete this sentence: 'Let he who is without sin . . .'"

Her response was, "Have a good time?" Leno then turned to a young man and asked: "Who, according to the Bible, was swallowed by a whale?" The young man smiled with confidence and said, "Oh, I know that one: Pinocchio!"

Now, we can laugh at that, but the hard reality is that many people today have a hole in their moral ozone. They know nothing about our moral tradition. They are morally confused. They are not spiritually mature enough to tell right from wrong.

A story attributed to Paul Harvey told the story of an old man who was a great admirer of democracy and public education. He had a great dream to bring those two things together in the creation of a new public college where the students would practice self-governance. There would be no rules or regulations. The goodwill and judgment of the students would run the college. After years of planning, the school was finally opened, and the old man was overjoyed. But as the months went by, the students proved time and time again that they were not the models of goodness and discipline and good judgment that the old man had envisioned. They skipped classes. They drank to excess. They wasted hours in frivolous pursuits.

Then one night, fourteen students disguised them-selves with masks, filled themselves with alcohol, and went on a rampage that ended in a brutal brawl. One student hit a professor with a brick, and another used a cane on his victim. In response, the college's trustees met in a special meeting. The old man, now eighty-two years old and very frail, was asked to address the student body. In his remarks, he recalled the lofty principles upon which the college had been founded. He said he had expected more—much more—from the students. He even confessed that this was the most painful event in his life. Suddenly, he stopped speaking. Tears welled up in his failing eyes. He was so overcome with grief that he sat down, unable to go on.

His audience was so touched that at the conclusion of the meeting the fourteen offenders stepped forward to admit their guilt. But they could not undo the damage already done. A strict code of conduct and numerous burdensome regulations were instituted at the college.

That college went on to become one of the great universities in America, but at that moment, the old man felt heartsick. His experiment hadn't gone the way he had planned. Why? Because he took for granted the one essential ingredient necessary for any democracy's success: the virtue and goodness of the people. Those young students weren't spiritually mature enough to realize that only a good and virtuous people can secure and maintain their freedom. A short time later, on the Fourth of July, the old man died. Engraved on his tombstone were these simple words:

> Thomas Jefferson
> Author of the Declaration of American Independence . . .
> and Father of the University of Virginia

In the 1830s, Alexis de Tocqueville came to America from France because he was so fascinated with the greatness of our country. He wanted to know what really made the dream work. There's an old adage that is often misattributed to de Tocqueville, but regardless of who first said or wrote these words, there is great meaning in them:

> I looked for the greatness of America in her fields and did not find it there. I looked for the greatness of America in her industries and did not find it there. But then I looked for the greatness of America in her churches and there I found it! America is great because America is good. If America ever loses her goodness, she will cease to be great.

Some years ago, newscaster Ted Koppel gave the commencement address at Duke University. He surprised his audience. He didn't talk about politics or international problems. Instead, he chose to speak on a subject that he thought those graduates needed to hear

and think about most of all: morality, personal morality!
And when he finished, he received a standing ovation!
In that speech, Ted Koppel said this:

> We have actually convinced ourselves that slogans will
> save us: "Shoot up if you must; but use a clean needle."
> . . . No! The answer is no. Not because it isn't cool or
> smart or because you might end up in jail or in an AIDS
> ward, but no because it's wrong, because we've spent
> 5,000 years as a race of rational human beings, trying to
> drag ourselves out of the primeval slime by searching
> for truth and moral absolutes. . . . In its purest form
> Truth is not a polite tap on the shoulder. It is a hallow-
> ing reproach. . . . What Moses brought down from
> Mount Sinai were not the Ten Suggestions, they are
> Commandments.
>
> (www.mediaresearch.org/mediawatch/1989/
> watch19890401.asp#analysis; accessed on 8-11-11)

That day at Duke University, Ted Koppel was saying
something we all need to hear, namely that the hope—
the only hope—of our nation and our world is that we
take seriously the truths of the Bible, appropriate them
to our lives, and live them daily. It's important to
remember that God's laws and commandments are not
given to us to put us in straitjackets but rather to help us
live life to the fullest. They are not there to hinder us
but to help us. Life is better when we love God and
other people. Life is better when we are honest and

loyal and truthful and kind and caring. God knew that, and that's why he gave us the great truths of the Bible to live by.

The point is clear: We've got to swing the pendulum back to goodness, because the goodness of the people is the lifeblood of a free society.

We Are in Danger of Becoming a Society of Splinter Groups

We have (in my opinion) way too many polarized cliques and vested interest groups who are concerned only about "feathering their nests," pressuring for the interests of their particular group with little or no concern for what is good for the nation, what is best for the country. As someone put it recently, "We have always been *E pluribus unum* [a Latin phrase meaning "Out of many, one"], but these days we seem to be more *pluribus* than *unum*." Too many groups today are forgetting that the *U* in USA stands for "United." It may sound like a cliché, but it is still profoundly true: United we stand; divided we fall.

I understand that we need groups to represent the varied interests of our people. But I also know that there are times when our vested interests and our partisan politics need to give way and take a backseat to what is best for the nation. I want us to be a united people, not a polarized people, not a fragmented people. President Dwight D. Eisenhower put it like this:

> A people that values its privileges above its principles soon loses both.
>
> (Dwight D. Eisenhower, Inaugural Address, January 20, 1953)

Whether Alexis de Tocqueville said it or whether it was someone else, the truth is that what makes America great is that Americans have a sense of community responsibility, a genuine compassion and desire for the well-being not just of themselves but of their neighbors. And so much of what we know about this kind of love, respect, and service to others, we learn in our churches.

We've got to swing the pendulum back from the proliferation of splinter groups because we are all in this together. United we stand; divided we fall.

We Are in Danger of Believing the Mistaken Notion That Freedom of Religion Means Freedom *from* Religion

People who believe this notion seem to think that religion should be avoided and eliminated from American life, and their position gets pushed to ridiculous extremes.

For example, in one of our northern states, the Supreme Court threw out the sentence of a murderer who killed a seventy-year-old woman with an ax on the ground that the prosecutor had unlawfully cited biblical law to the jury in his summation.

A few years ago in one of our western cities, a fourth-grade girl was told by her schoolteacher that she could not wear a cross on her necklace.

In a Midwestern town some time ago, the word *God* was discovered in a second-grade phonics textbook. The children were told to strike it out because it is against the law to mention God in a public school.

A town in Middle America not long ago blocked a private Catholic hospital from erecting a cross on its smokestack because members of the city council said some local residents would be offended.

And then, look at what's happening in the entertainment world. Noted film critic Michael Medved was so concerned about it that he produced a video documentary entitled *Hollywood vs. Religion*, in which he showed how the movie industry has changed over the years and how they now seem to go out of their way to take potshots at religion.

In earlier days, religious leaders were portrayed as strong heroes like Spencer Tracy in *Boys Town*, but today in film and television many religious leaders are portrayed as weak, wimpy, narrow-minded, and sometimes even evil. Medved says that the creators of such works often will say, "Oh, we are not a thermostat; we are a thermometer. We don't set the climate, we just register the climate." Well, let me tell you something—don't you believe that for a minute! Hollywood and others are setting the climate, and too often it is a climate not favorable to religion. Those who think freedom of religion means freedom *from* religion are wrong.

Now, please don't misunderstand me. I know that we have great diversity in our nation. I know that we are multicultural and multiethnic. I saw a figure indicating that we have more than one thousand different religious groups in our country. I know that there is a need for respect and understanding with regard to our religious differences. But I also know about our faith heritage as a nation. A nation's identity is shaped by morality, and morality comes from faith.

How can we debate serious ethical issues such as nuclear arms or the death penalty or drug addiction without making references to religion? How can U.S. children be truly educated without any reference to our spiritual heritage? It's impossible! We need some common sense here. So much of who we are goes back to the great lessons of the Bible. So much of the civilizing process is rooted in our doctrines of faith. So many of our present-day laws go back to the Ten Commandments. And so much of the best of what we are—in my opinion—goes back to the life and teachings of Jesus.

The point is this: We've got to swing the pendulum back to goodness and unity and faith. Goodness, unity, and faith; if you stop to think about it, this would be a good time for us as a nation and for us as individuals to once again hear the voice of the prophet Micah saying those powerful words that are just as true today as they were when he spoke them in the eighth century B.C.:

> What does the Lord require of you
> but to do justice, and to love kindness,
> and to walk humbly with your God?

CHAPTER NINE

I Hear the Voice of Mary Saying, "Let It Be to Me According to Your Word"

Scripture: Luke 1:39-45

His name was Joey. Joey was nine years old and in the fourth grade. He was so excited because his teacher, Miss Thompson, had chosen him to be in the annual Christmas play. Joey was going to be one of the Christmas angels, and he was more than a little nervous, because he had a speaking part in the play, and memorizing lines was not his strong suit. He had only one line, but Miss Thompson told him that it was one of the most important lines in the whole story.

Joey was to play the angel of Christmas, and at the most dramatic moment in the pageant, he was to say:

"Behold, I bring you glad tidings of great joy." This was a problem for Joey, because he didn't know what those words meant. He had never in his whole life said the word *behold*, and the words *glad tidings* were also not to be found anywhere in his nine-year-old vocabulary.

Miss Thompson sensed Joey's frustration, and she said to him, "Joey, simply imagine that you have just heard the most wonderful news, and you have run to tell your friends all about it. That's what 'Behold, I bring you glad tidings of great joy' means." Joey took in her explanation, and he went to work. Finally he mastered the line, and he could say it with dramatic flair and boldness: "Behold, I bring you glad tidings of great joy!"

And when the night of the big performance came, Joey was ready! At least, he was ready until the curtains opened and he saw all those people out there, and then there were those bright spotlights shining directly in his face. Joey got a classic case of stage fright, and his mind went completely blank! For the life of him, he could not remember his line. Not a word of it. But he did remember what Miss Thompson had told him about running to tell his friends some wonderful news, so when it came time for his line, instead of saying, "Behold, I bring you glad tidings of great joy!" Joey blurted out, "Boy, oh boy, do I have good news for *you!*" The audience laughed loudly and gave Joey a standing ovation!

A few people got upset with Joey, because they felt that he had ruined the Christmas play. But more (many, many more) loved it and felt that Joey's blurted-out words were the highlight of the pageant, and that through a little child it had happened: Christmas had come once again!

Joey's unusual performance actually happened years ago, but to this day in that community, when the people gather for the annual Christmas play, they all talk about Joey and how on that night long ago, Joey got the words wrong, but the spirit right when he shouted out with great enthusiasm, "Boy, oh boy, do I have good news for *you!*"

Well, Joey was right, wasn't he? Christmas does have good news for us, incredible news, amazing news, the greatest news this world has ever heard.

Christmas also has some wonderful lessons about life to teach us. We see that, for example, in the first chapter of Luke's Gospel in this beautiful scene where Mary, who is to become the mother of Jesus, goes to visit her older cousin Elizabeth, who also is expecting. Elizabeth, even though she is quite old to be having a baby, will soon miraculously deliver a baby boy who will grow up to be John the Baptist, the forerunner of the Messiah, the one who will prepare the way for the coming of Jesus Christ. God blessed both Mary and Elizabeth with miracle births, that he might bless the world with the miracle of Christmas.

Notice this: God first sends an angel to Elizabeth and her husband, Zechariah, then to Mary and Joseph, then to the shepherds, and in each case, the angel says, in essence, "Boy, oh boy, do I have good news for *you!*"

Let's look together at this poignant passage in Luke 1 where these two expectant mothers (one quite old and one quite young) get together to talk about the miraculous things that are happening and to affirm and support each other. Boy, oh boy, is there good news here for you and me! Let me show you what I mean.

Look at the Good News of Christmas Found in the Faith of Mary

Her strong, unflinching, unwavering faith is amazing. Some years ago, a new Christmas song was written entitled "Mary, Did You Know?" The song was written by Mark Lowry and Buddy Greene, and several different musical artists have recorded it. In the lyrics, the composer is asking Mary if she really knew and understood the amazing thing that was happening. Did she really comprehend who her baby boy was? Did she realize what her Son would do in the world and for the world? Did she know already the good he would do, the miracles he would perform, the good news he would bring? And then the song concludes with these powerful words: "[Mary] Did you know that your baby boy is heaven's perfect Lamb? / This sleeping child you're holding is the great I Am."

Well, what do you think? How much did Mary know? Let's go back to the story in Luke and find out.

There is so much to learn from Mary. She has so much to teach us about real faith. When we see her so beautifully portrayed in Christmas pageants and on Christmas cards and in Nativity scenes, she looks so serene and lovely and the whole matter appears so simple and easy.

But—think realistically about it for a moment. Consider realistically what Mary went through. It must have been incredibly difficult to deal with:

- the whisperings behind her back;
- the pointed fingers;
- the false accusations;
- the raised eyebrows;
- the questions;
- the gossip;
- the criticism;
- the family pressures;
- the crude jokes;

- the cruel laughter;
- the poverty;
- the heavy taxes;
- the hard journey to Bethlehem (see Luke 2:1-7);
- the birth in a stable, with no doctor, no midwife, no medicine, and no anesthetic—nothing but faith in God!

Mary was just a teenaged girl from a poor family who lived in an obscure village, which itself was under the rule of a despised foreign power. Then one day, out of the blue, an angel came to her with a message from the Lord: "Do not be afraid, Mary, for you have found favor with God. And behold, you will conceive in your womb and bear a son, and you shall call his name Jesus. He will be great, and will be called the Son of the Most High" (Luke 1:30-32 RSV). And all of this was going to happen without Mary's ever being intimate with any man.

Now, be honest. Would you have believed that? The remarkable thing is that Mary did! That's real faith, isn't it? She was willing to hear God's word, obey God's will, and entrust the future in God's hands, even though it put her in an awkward, difficult, complicated situation. How would she explain this? How would she communicate this to her parents? How would she tell

Joseph? They were legally betrothed. They had not yet consummated their marriage, but they were considered "as good as married," and in those days when you became formally engaged as they were, the only way you could be separated was through divorce. How could she tell Joseph, that she was going to have a baby, and how would he handle it? And what would the neighbors say?

It was a tough situation for Mary, and most of us would have asked the Lord to find someone else to do this job. But not Mary. She did not know what was ahead for her and her son—not a lot of specifics, not a lot of details—but her answer to the angel was a model of real faith, "I am the handmaid of the Lord," she said. "Let it be to me according to your word" (Luke 1:38 RSV). Or in other words, what Mary said was, "I am the Lord's servant. O Lord, thy will be done. Use me, O Lord, as you will. I trust you completely." What a powerful portrait of faith we see in Mary!

Let me ask you something. Do you have faith like that? Can you say, "Thy will be done, O Lord," and really mean it, really trust God like Mary did? Is your faith that strong? That's something to think about, isn't it?

The faith of Mary: that's number one.

Look at the Good News of Christmas in the Encouragement of Elizabeth

In Luke 1, when Mary comes to visit her older cousin Elizabeth, isn't it beautiful how Elizabeth responds? No jealousy, no skepticism, no cynicism, no suspicious questions—just loving affirmation, positive reinforcement, an "I love you," "I'm so happy for you," "I'm so proud of you," "I'm here for you" (see Luke 1:39-45, 56). We all need someone like that.

When I was a teenager, my older cousin Marie filled that role for me. She was twenty-five years older than me, and no matter what, she was always glad to see me, always glad to listen to me, always loving, always upbeat, always affirming, always encouraging. I could bring my joys and sorrows, my victories and disappointments to Marie, and I knew before I said a word just how she would respond: with love and encouragement. I have wonderful memories of Marie and her wisdom, the ways in which she always gave me the positive reinforcement I needed.

Some years ago at a university in the Midwest, some students in a psychology class were studying the power of positive reinforcement—the impact it has on a person when you give encouragement and the debilitating effect that comes when positive reinforcement is withheld. The psychology professor was called out of the room for

a few moments one day. Now, leaving psychology
students alone even for a few minutes is risky business,
as the professor soon found out. The students decided to
have some fun with the professor and, at the same time,
to test his theories about positive reinforcement.

The professor was in the habit of pacing back and
forth across the front of the classroom as he lectured.
So the students decided, without the professor's knowl-
edge, to do this: Every time the professor moved toward
the radiator in the classroom, they would give him dramatic positive reinforcement. They would say, "Yes! All
right! Amen!" They would applaud and smile and nod
and take notes like crazy! With verbal expression and
body language they affirmed and encouraged him as he
walked toward the radiator.

But when he moved away from the radiator, the students would do the opposite. They would moan and
groan and yawn and stretch and put their pencils down.
They would look out the window or nod off as though
they were about to fall asleep, and they would look and
act as if they were bored to tears. They never told the
professor what they were doing, and he never figured it
out. But by the end of the week, he was giving his en-
tire lecture sitting on the radiator!

We all need it, positive reinforcement, and this is one
of the great messages of Christmas. God, through the

gift of the Christ Child, reaches out to us with love and encouragement and affirmation, and he wants us to live in that spirit, as Elizabeth did. God wants us to celebrate one another and to give one another the positive reinforcement, love, and encouragement we all need.

How is it with you right now? Are you a child of faith like Mary? Are you a child of encouragement like Elizabeth?

Look at the Good News of Christmas in the Action of God

The gracious, loving, forgiving, seeking, saving action of God: This is the good news of Christmas! God will not give up on us. God will not desert us. God will not let us go. God comes to where we are, looking for us with his amazing grace and his sacrificial, redemptive love.

In 1989 an earthquake hit Armenia, and thirty thousand people lost their lives. One area hit especially hard had an elementary school in it. After the tremors had stopped, a father of one of the students raced to the school to check on his son. When the father arrived on the scene, he was stunned to see that the school building had been leveled. Looking at the mass of stones and rubble, he remembered a promise he had made to his little boy, Arman. He had told him, "No matter what happens, Arman, I'll always be there for you." Remembering his promise, he found the area closest to his son's classroom and began to pull back the rocks. Others had also come, and they said to the man, "It's too late. You know they are all gone. No one could survive that! You can't help them now." Even a policeman urged him to give up and go on home.

But that father refused to quit. For eight hours, then sixteen, then thirty-two, and then thirty-six hours, he continued to dig through the rubble. His hands were raw and his energy gone, but he would not give up. Finally, after thirty-eight wrenching hours, he pulled back a boulder, and he heard voices. He recognized his son's voice. He called out to him, "Arman! Arman!" And a voice answered him, "Dad, it's me!" And then the boy said, "I told the other kids not to worry. I told them if you were alive, you would come and save me, and when you saved me, they would be saved, too. Because you promised, 'No matter what, I'll always be there for you.' I knew you would never give up or let me down."

This is the good news of Christmas, isn't it? God comes into the rubble of our lives and seeks us out and saves us. We see the miracle of Christmas in the faith of Mary and in the encouragement of Elizabeth, but most of all, we see it in the saving action of God.

CHAPTER TEN

I Hear the Voice of Jesus Saying, "Love One Another as I Have Loved You"

SCRIPTURE: JOHN 15:12-14

The noted writer Norman Cousins wrote a book called *The Healing Heart*. It was written out of his own personal experience of having and surviving a heart attack. In the book, he gives great accolades to the highly proficient and multitalented doctors of our time. But he also states that while some doctors today are brilliant technicians, brilliant scientists, they are not all "people persons." Many, he says, have no training at all in the art of communication, no training at all in relating warmly to their patients, and consequently, he says, "they don't realize how the hospital patients look so forward to their visits and hang on their every word."

I'm sure that Norman Cousins had a point that medical schools should take seriously, but I must hurry to tell you that I have not found that to be true with the doctors I know in my city and church. With so many of them, you get the best of both worlds! You get a doctor with not only a bright mind and talented hands but also a warm and compassionate heart. You get a physician and a pastor all rolled into one!

A case in point was documented for me some time ago by a doctor, an acquaintance of mine, who had a moving and touching experience with one of his patients. The doctor is a highly respected heart surgeon, and he had helped this patient with her medical problem. And knowing this doctor as I do, I'm sure that he also had befriended her with his warm and compassionate Christian spirit. To express her gratitude, the patient gave her doctor a gift. The gift was a beautiful ceramic heart (a fitting gift for a heart doctor), and attached to the gift was a beautiful message, a prayer-poem entitled "Heartprints," an often-quoted poem whose author was not identified. Here are the words:

> Whatever our hands touch—
> We leave fingerprints!

On walls, on furniture,
On doorknobs, dishes, books,
As we touch we leave our identity.

O God, wherever I go today,
Help me to leave heartprints!
Heartprints of compassion,
Of understanding and love.
Heartprints of kindness
And genuine concern.

May my heart touch a lonely neighbor,
Or a runaway daughter,
Or an anxious mother,
Or, perhaps, a dear friend!

Lord, send me out today
To leave heartprints.
And if anyone should say,
"I felt your touch,"
May that one sense thy love
Touching through me.

Some years later after the doctor had shared with me this touching experience and this powerful prayer-poem, I was asked to conduct a graveside memorial service for one of my neighbors. She was a good friend and an Episcopal priest. She had grown up in our United Methodist church, but when she married a fine man who was a devout Episcopalian, she joined his church and a few years later she became an Episcopalian priest. She had served for some years with great distinction until health problems had pushed her into an early retirement. Those same health problems eventually took her life.

At the conclusion of her graveside service, I shared with her family the story about the heart surgeon and the prayer-poem he had been given. I read that prayer-poem aloud and commented that their loved one's life had been such a beautiful symbol of this prayer-poem, because she had indeed left "heartprints" everywhere she had been. As I stood beside her gravesite and read the prayer-poem aloud as the closing prayer of the memorial service, I could tell that the family was greatly moved by the story and the prayer-poem. They were all crying and smiling and touching their hearts at the same time. After the service, they all rushed to hug me and thank me for concluding with that prayer-poem. It had meant so much to them. Then, the deceased woman's parents told me something that I didn't know: The woman who had given the ceramic heart and the prayer-poem to my heart-surgeon friend was in fact their daughter! What a moment that was! It was a "God moment" that will stay with me forever.

That prayer poem, "Heartprints," simply underscores something the Bible has been telling us all along, namely, that there is nothing in the world more powerful than the healing power of love. Sometimes we forget that or wonder about it, maybe even doubt it. We want to put our faith in military power and intellectual pursuits and scientific advances and economic strength and international alliances and political clout.

But over and over, the Scriptures tell us that love is the answer, that love is the will of God for us, that love is the single most authentic sign of discipleship, that love is the hope of the world. Here in John 15, we see it again. Jesus said, "This is my commandment, that you love one another as I have loved you. No one has greater love than this, to lay down one's life for one's friends. You are my friends if you do what I command you" (verses 12-14).

Jesus was the Great Physician, and he knew full well about the healing power of love. Let's look at that now, the incredible, amazing, awesome, healing power of love. Dr. Karl Menninger, the well-known psychiatrist, once said that he believes the most tragic word in human language today is the word unloved. Feeling unloved; there's nothing worse than that, nothing more devastating than that, nothing more destructive than that. Dr. Menninger went on to say that on the other hand, "Love has the power to cure people—both the ones who give it and the ones who receive it."

(www.menningerclinic.com/about/early-history.htm; accessed 8-11-11). And he's right. Love can cure. The heartprints of love can restore and mend and heal. Let me be more specific.

Love Has the Power to Heal Us Physically

Scientific research is now confirming what many of us have suspected all along: that love plays a big part in the healing of a hurting body.

Roy Angell told the story about a particularly affectionate puppy that liked to hang out around a sanitarium. A doctor at the sanitarium decided to try an experiment on the pup. She made a small incision on the puppy's leg. Then she bandaged it. Finally, she instructed those at the sanitarium to feed the puppy when he was hungry, but not to show him any affection physically or verbally. The change in the little dog was quick and dramatic. Whereas before he had always been energetic, frisky, happy, and friendly, he now seemed quite forlorn and pitiful. Even more significant, six weeks later the incision on his leg had not healed.

The doctor then instructed everyone at the sanitarium to do just the opposite—to lavish love on the little puppy, to speak kindly to him, to hold him, pet him, stroke him, and love him. Soon the puppy was frisky and happy and energetic again. And the incision healed very quickly. The point is clear: The healing streams that lie within the body, which may be energized and activated by the power of love, are potent indeed, more so perhaps than we even realize.

A few years ago in Sweden, a nurse working in a government hospital was assigned to an elderly woman patient. This patient was a tough case. She had not spoken a word in three years. The other nurses disliked her and tried to avoid her as much as they could. Basically, they ignored her. But the new nurse decided to try "unconditional love." The patient rocked all day in a rocking chair. So one day, the nurse pulled up a rocking chair beside the patient and just rocked along with her, and loved her. Occasionally, the nurse would reach over and gently touch and pat the hand of the woman.

After just a few days of this, the patient suddenly opened her eyes, turned, and said to the nurse, "You're so kind." The next day, she talked more, and incredibly, two weeks later, the patient was well enough to leave the hospital and go home! Of course, it doesn't always work like that, but studies are accumulating that show, without question, that love has healing power.

Take for example the poet Elizabeth Barrett. She was an invalid for many years, unable to leave her home. But then, one day she was visited by a man named Robert Browning. It was love at first sight. In just a few visits, he brought her so much joy and happiness that she showed marked recovery. Eventually, she was strong enough to elope and move with him to Italy!

Love can heal us physically! No wonder people were healed by coming into physical contact with Jesus. He was love incarnate. And that's what he is calling us to be today—love made flesh. Love personified. Love lived out.

This is the first point. Love can heal bodies. Love can heal us physically.

Love Has the Power to Heal Us Emotionally

Some years ago, when I was serving a church in another state, a man and his wife came to see me one day. They were burdened, worried, troubled. It was obvious. I could tell that they both had been crying. The man spoke first: "It's our daughter, Betty. She's eighteen years old now, and we are worried sick about her. She has absolutely no self-esteem at all, and she has gotten a reputation around town."

"Reputation?" I asked. "What do you mean?"

"Well," said the man painfully, "her self-esteem is so low that any time any man pays attention to her . . ." (his voice trailed off, and he began to sob). Then the man's wife said it bluntly: "Jim, she can't say no to any man, and now, she has this horrible reputation. It's all over town. We're worried sick, and we're scared. We're at the end of our rope. We don't know what to do with her. She's emotionally ill. She needs help."

Well, I met with Betty, and they were right about her self-esteem. It was nonexistent. She walked all slumped over. Her hair was dirty and scraggly, her clothes unkempt. She could not look me in the eye. Most of the time she stared at the floor, and when she looked up, her eyes darted like a scared rabbit. She was in a pitiful state. I brought in a psychiatrist. We both worked with her, but to be honest we didn't make much progress at all. It seemed hopeless.

But then, the most amazing thing happened. A new young man named Jerry moved to town. He was the son of a pastor, and he fell in love with Betty. He said, "Betty, I know about your past. I know about your reputation. I know the names they call you. I've heard all the rumors, but I also know that I love you, and you are so beautiful to me!" He kept telling her, "I love you, and you are so beautiful." And pretty soon, she started believing him. She began to stand up straight. She put on a little makeup. She combed her hair. She bought some new clothes. And she did something else I'd never seen her do before: She started smiling!

Not long after, I performed their wedding, and then shortly thereafter I moved away to another city. A couple of years later, I was invited to come back to that church to preach one Sunday morning. As I walked toward the sanctuary, I passed through the children's building, and I saw Jerry coming out of a Sunday school classroom. He had been teaching a children's class. With him was a gorgeous woman. She looked like a model—tall, stately, poised, radiant—and I thought: *Oh my goodness, Jerry has left Betty and found somebody else.* But I was wrong!

As I drew closer to them, I realized that the gorgeous, radiant, confident woman who had been helping Jerry teach the children in Sunday school was none other than Betty herself! I could hardly believe my eyes, and deep down in my heart I hummed the Doxology! Betty had been transformed. She had been restored. She had been made well. She had been healed by love!

Love has the power to heal us, both physically and emotionally.

Love Has the Power to Heal Us Spiritually

A well-known speaker started off his seminar by holding up a crisp, new $20 bill. There were two hundred people in the room. The speaker asked them, "How many of you would like to have this $20 bill?" Hands went up all over the room. Then the speaker said, "I'm going to give this $20 bill to one of you, but first let me do this." He proceeded to crumple the $20 bill, and then he held it up and said, "Who wants it now?" Hands went up everywhere. "Well," he replied, "What if I do this?" He dropped it on the ground and stepped on it, and started to grind it into the floor with his shoe. He picked it up and held it up for all to see. It was crumpled and smudged and dirty, and he said, "Who wants it now?" Still, hands went up all over the place. Then the speaker said, "My friends, you have just learned a very valuable lesson. No matter what I did to the money, you still wanted it because it did not decrease in value. No matter how smudged and rumpled it became, it was still worth $20."

Many times in our lives, we get knocked around—dropped, crumpled, smudged, and ground into the dirt—by the decisions we make and the circumstances that come our way. And sometimes we feel as though we are worthless and used up and of no account. But no matter what has happened or what will happen, you will never lose your value in God's eyes. To God, dirty or clean, crumpled or finely creased, you are still priceless! The psalmist in Psalm 17:8 asks God to guard him as the apple of God's eye. And God will always keep us as the apple of his eye, not because we are good, but because *God* is good. That is God's amazing grace, and that is the only way spiritual healing can happen.

In his book *Come Share the Being,* Bob Benson writes about God's incredible grace and the amazing ways in which God shares himself with us. He writes:

> Do you remember when they had old-fashioned Sunday School picnics? It was before air-conditioning. They said, "We'll meet at Sycamore Lodge in Shelby Park at 4:30 Saturday. You bring your supper and we'll furnish the tea."
>
> But you came home at the last minute and when you got ready to pack your lunch, all you could find in the refrigerator was one dried up piece of baloney and just enough mustard in the bottom of the jar so that you got it all over your knuckles trying to get it out. And there were just two stale pieces of bread. So, you made your baloney sandwich and wrapped it in some brown bag and went to the picnic. And when it came time to eat, you sat at the end of a table and spread out your sandwich.
>
> But the folks next to you—the lady was a good cook and she had worked all day and they had fried chicken and baked beans and potato salad and homemade rolls and sliced tomatoes and pickles and olives and celery and topped it off with two big homemade chocolate pies. And they spread it all out beside you . . . And there you were with your stale baloney sandwich. But they said to you, "Why don't we put it all together?" "Oh no, I couldn't do that. I just couldn't even think of it," you murmured embarrassedly. "Oh, come on. There's plenty of chicken and plenty of pie and plenty of everything—and we just love baloney sandwiches!" "Let's put it all together." And so

you did . . . and there you sat—eating like a king when you came like a pauper.

The point is obvious: We bring our little, and God brings his much, and in his Amazing Grace, God says "Let's put it all together." If we will only accept it in faith, God has a banquet for us when we are hungry. God has healing for us when we are hurting. God can satisfy the hollow emptiness within us. God can make the wounded whole. God can heal the sin-sick soul, through the power, the healing power, of his love!

What a great word to hear today and every day, the eloquent voice of Jesus saying, "Love is the most powerful thing in the world, so love one another as I have loved you."

CHAPTER ELEVEN

I Hear the Voice of Paul Saying, "The Greatest of These Is Love"

SCRIPTURE: 1 CORINTHIANS 13

Some friends gave me a copy of a wonderful item entitled "The World According to Student Bloopers" (www.cse.unsw.edu.au/~norman/Jokes-file/Student Bloopers.htm ; accessed 8-11-11). Compiled by Richard Lederer of St. Paul's School, it's a humorous list of student bloopers collected by teachers of young students from all across the United States, with actual quotes from student essays and tests.

One student wrote this: "The inhabitants of ancient Egypt were called mummies. They lived in the Sarah Dessert and traveled by Camelot."

Another gave this answer on a Bible quiz: "Jacob was a man in the Bible who stole his brother's birthmark."

One student said: "The Greeks . . . had myths. A myth is a female moth."

Still another wrote this: "Socrates was a famous Greek teacher who went around giving people advice. They killed him. Socrates died from an overdose of wedlock."

One student gave this definition: "History call[s] people Romans because they never stayed in one place for very long. . . .

"Nero was a cruel tyranny who would torture his poor subjects by playing the fiddle to them."

And look at this one: "William Tell . . . shot an arrow through an apple while standing on his son's head."

Or how about this: "Gravity was invented by Isaac Walton. It is chiefly noticeable in the Autumn, when the apples are [falling] off the trees."

One student of American History gave this description of Benjamin Franklin: "[Benjamin] Franklin had gone to Boston carrying all his clothes in his pocket and a loaf of bread under each arm. He invented electricity by rubbing cats backwards and declared 'a horse divided against itself cannot stand.' Franklin died in 1790 and is still dead."

And finally, another student had this to say about Abraham Lincoln: "He was born in a log cabin which he built with his own hands."

It is obvious from these classic student bloopers that sometimes we miss the message. Sometimes we stop short of the full truth, and consequently we end up with distorted or strange answers. The plain fact is that sometimes we "sort of" learn something but don't quite get it right. If we are not careful, we can just play around the edges of truth and somehow miss the main point.

This is precisely what the message of the apostle Paul in 1 Corinthians 13 is all about. Here, Paul is underscoring the crucial truth, the main point.

The apostle Paul had founded the church in Corinth around A.D. 50, and he had stayed with the people there for about eighteen months. But then when he moved on to work in Ephesus, he kept getting these disquieting reports of trouble in the Corinthian church. As long as he had been there with them, everything had gone nicely; but when he left, all kinds of problems broke out. Conflicts and cliques, divisions and dissensions, party strife and power struggles literally were tearing the church apart. Jealousy, self-righteousness, greed, hostility, and arrogance were running rampant, and all in the name of religion!

Can you imagine that? How could this happen? Well, the Corinthians had gotten a taste of religion, but they had missed the main point! They were playing around the edges and missing the main message! So, like a father teaching his children, the apostle Paul must deal with the Corinthians. First, he examines their problems (for the first twelve chapters of his letter to them, he dissects their mistakes and misunderstandings); and then Paul shows them a better way!

"Now, *look!* Here it is!" he says to them. "This is what it's all about! Here is the secret! You want the key to life? Well, here it is for you!" And he launches into 1 Corinthians 13, which is sometimes referred to as "the Love Chapter":

> If I speak in the tongues of mortals and of angels, but do not have love, I am a noisy gong or a clanging cymbal. And if I have prophetic powers, and understand all mysteries and all knowledge, and if I have all faith so, as to remove mountains, but do not have love, I am nothing. If I give away all my possessions, and if I hand over my body so that I may boast, but do not have not love, I gain nothing.
>
> Love is patient; love is kind; love is not envious or boastful or arrogant or rude. It does not insist on its own way; it is not irritable or resentful; it does not rejoice in wrongdoing, but rejoices in the truth. It bears all things, believes all things, hopes all things, endures all things.
>
> Love never ends. . . . And now faith, hope, and love abide, these three; and the greatest of these is love." (1 Corinthians 13:1-8a, 13)

Powerful, moving, majestic words, but what is Paul really communicating here? He is saying the same thing Jesus said again and again: Love is the key, the secret, the answer. Love is the one thing that is always right. Love is the major ingredient in a happy family. Love is the most authentic sign of discipleship and spiritual maturity. Love is the single-most powerful thing in the world. Love is the most dramatic evidence of God's powerful presence in our lives. If we miss love we miss the main point, and we miss God!

So, what better thing could we do than think together about this question: How do we teach our children to be loving persons? I asked a number of people that question recently, and it's interesting, they all gave the same answer. They all said, "By example!" That's a good answer. Let's break that down a bit and see if we can find ourselves or our children somewhere between the lines.

We Can Teach Our Children to Be Loving by the Example of Respect

We can teach our children to have respect for others and to have respect for themselves as persons.

Recently I was standing in line in a supermarket. There was a family in front of me who got into a rather heated argument. I never cease to be amazed at how some people talk to their children. As I overheard these parents unload this vicious verbal attack on their child, I thought to myself that they wouldn't talk to a roach like that, with those ugly words and in that hostile, venomous tone of voice.

Horrible expletives, dirty names, profane accusations, nasty insinuations, and angry put-downs were all aimed directly at a tired little boy who just wanted a five-cent piece of bubblegum. Maybe he didn't need the bubblegum, but even when we say no, we can say it with respect, can't we? We always need to remember that every child is a child of God, a human being, a person of integrity and worth, a person for whom Christ came and died. One of the ways we teach our children how to be loving persons is by being patient with them, understanding of them, and respectful toward them in every stage of their lives.

I ran across an article that had appeared in a Dutch magazine. It was called "How Fathers Mature," but it's really about the many different transitions children go through over the years as they assess their fathers. See if any of this sounds familiar:

> I'm 4 years old, and my Daddy can do anything.
> I'm 7 years old, and my Dad knows a whole lot.
> I'm 9 years old, and Dad doesn't know quite everything.
> I'm 12 years old, and Dad just doesn't understand.
> I'm 14 years old, and Dad is so old-fashioned.

I'm 17 years old, and the man is out of touch and out to lunch.

I'm 25 years old, and Dad's okay.

I'm 30 years old: I wonder what Dad would think about this.

I'm 35 years old: I must get Dad's input first.

I'm 50 years old and wonder what would Dad have thought about that?

I'm 60 years old, and I sure wish I could talk it over with Dad once more.

They will go through stages and they may go off on tangents, but if we respect our children and if they see us treating every person we meet with dignity and respect, with kindness and courtesy, they will "go to school on us" and they will learn how to love. Most often they will work through the stages, the fads, the peer pressures, and the transitions and eventually, more often than not, they will come back to the values of their parents, to the principles and the standards of their home, and to the art of love.

So, that's number one: We can teach our children to love by the example of respect.

We Can Teach Our Children to Be Loving Persons by the Example of Sacrifice

People who have been forced by circumstances to sacrifice for each other have a special tenderness toward each other. Two Army buddies who have been forced to share their rations or their canteen of water in a difficult time never forget each other. There is something about sacrificing together that creates love.

A few years ago, I spoke at a college graduation exercise. Something happened that day that I will never forget. One young woman, when she received her diploma, instead of going back to her seat broke out of line, walked about halfway into the audience, and handed the diploma to her parents. Then she hugged them both tightly, and they all cried together tears of joy. Her parents looked a little tired. Their clothes were not the latest style. I never knew for sure why that young graduate did that, but I suspect that through that act she was saying, "We did it together. You deserve this too. I have come to this place because of you. I know how you've sacrificed for me." It was a powerful demonstration of love. Sacrifice creates love!

First, there is respect; and second, there is sacrifice.

We Can Teach Our Children to Be Loving Persons by the Example of Christ

The best thing we can do for our children is introduce them to Jesus Christ. If we help them accept Christ into their lives as a powerful presence, then we have done the best thing we can do for them. If they catch his spirit from us, then that, more than anything else, will make them genuine, loving persons. But it has to be more than a vague nod in his direction. It has to be more than a spiritual "tip of the hat." It has to be a personal relationship, a constant and ongoing closeness, a warm and lively friendship, a deep and unshakable commitment.

During World War II, a young man went overseas. A few days after he left, his wife gave birth to a baby boy. For three years that young soldier served in the South Pacific, and he and his little son never saw each other. The wife tried to bridge the problem of separation by practicing a little ritual each night as she put the child to bed. Each evening they would put on his pajamas, kneel beside the bed to say their prayers, and then the little boy would run over to a framed picture of his father on the bedside table, kiss the picture of his dad, and then run back and tumble into bed. This nightly ritual went on for three years.

Then the day finally came when the war was over and the father returned home. That night for the first time, the father got to participate in the bedtime ritual. He helped his son put on his pajamas. Then mother, father, and son knelt together beside the bed for prayer, and when the prayers were completed, the boy's mother said, "Now you can kiss your father goodnight." Can you imagine what happened? That's right. The little boy ran over to the nightstand, kissed his father's picture, then ran back and tumbled into bed, leaving his dad standing there with open, empty arms!

Now, of course over time the little boy understood. He came to know his dad as a person, as a living presence and not just a picture. But that's a parable for us, isn't it? Many people today in their religious experience are still merely "kissing the picture." They haven't really accepted the Living Christ into their lives. They don't really know him personally yet. They just kiss the picture.

If we want our children to be loving persons, we can teach them how to love by showing them respect and sacrifice and by introducing them to Christ. He will not only teach them to love, he will love them through and he will love through them!

Every day of our lives, we would benefit incredibly by hearing the powerful voice of the apostle Paul saying, "Faith, hope, and love abide, these three; and the greatest of these is love."

CHAPTER TWELVE

I Hear the Voice of Mary Magdalene Saying, "He Is Risen!"

SCRIPTURE: JOHN 20:16-21

Have you heard the story about the woman from Houston who some years ago made a trip to Los Angeles? While there, she went into an ice cream shop and ordered an ice cream cone. While she was waiting for her ice cream to be prepared, she glanced casually to her right and almost fainted—sitting there at the counter right beside her was the noted actor Paul Newman! She had always been crazy about Paul Newman. He was her heartthrob, her dreamboat—and there he was, close enough to touch! She couldn't believe it. She was so excited and so nervous, but she decided to be strong and to maintain her composure. After all, she didn't want to act silly or do anything dumb in front of Paul Newman!

The woman paid for her ice cream and (discreetly fanning her flushed face) went outside, proud of how disciplined and poised she had been. Out on the sidewalk, however, she realized that she didn't have her ice cream cone. She was so embarrassed, but she thought, *I wanted that ice cream cone. I paid for it, and I'm going to go back in there to get it!* Back inside, she told the clerk, "I didn't get my ice cream cone. I paid for it, but I didn't get it."

"Well, I gave it to you," answered the clerk.

"You can see," she said, "that I don't have it."

At that moment, Paul Newman spoke up and said, "Lady, you put it in your purse!"

Whether this is a true story or an urban legend, I don't know; but either way, it's a good story! It is funny, and it has a great surprise ending. And we do love stories with great surprise endings. This is what the Easter story is about, isn't it? It has the most glorious, magnificent, incredible, joyous surprise ending.

On the third day following Jesus' crucifixion on the cross, Mary Magdalene came to Jesus' tomb on Easter morning looking for a dead body, but she was surprised by a risen Lord. She came to the tomb trudging slowly along, mourning the painful loss of her Lord, but she returned from the tomb that morning excitedly running and jumping and full of surprise, shouting with joy, "He is risen! He is risen!" She came to the tomb feeling the agony of defeat, but she was surprised by the thrill of victory.

And, talk about surprises—look at what Easter morning did to Good Friday's cross. Easter redeemed the cross—*changed it—converted it!* Think about it: Why are we so strangely fascinated by the cross today? Why do we as Christians display the cross and wear the cross and kneel before the cross? Why do we sing, in such startlingly illogical fashion, words such as "in the cross of Christ I glory"? How can we glory in a cross? Do you remember what the cross was like on Good Friday?

In the first place, the cross was *great suffering*—excruciating pain, cruel punishment, prolonged agony. They mocked Jesus, beat him, made vulgar jokes about him, called him filthy names, slapped him in the face, and nailed him to a cross. Crucifixion was a horrible thing, a bloody, dusty, sweaty, sordid, nasty business. It was intense suffering.

Not only that, but the cross was also *public shame*. That's why Jesus was compelled to carry his own cross through the busy, crowded streets of Jerusalem. That's why the execution was done in a public place, where the people could see it, and why Jesus was stripped of his clothing. That's why he was nailed helpless to a cross, where he was the object of taunts and indignities from passersby. All of this was done to subject the crucified victim to public shame and to ridicule him. It was suffering. It was shame.

But also, the cross was *crime prevention*. This was Rome's intimidating way of saying, "You'd better stay in line. You'd better toe the mark or this could very well happen to you!"

It's not a very pretty picture, is it? So, how can we "glory in a cross," the emblem of suffering and shame and crime prevention? Isn't that like singing a hymn to the hangman's noose, the electric chair, or the gas chamber? Why are we so powerfully drawn to the cross?

The answer is because of Easter. The reason we can celebrate and love the cross is because we stand on the Easter side of Good Friday. We stand on the Resurrection side of the cross. We see the cross through Easter eyes, and we know that even there in suffering, shame, and torment, Jesus was somehow bringing a great victory.

Jesus came off the cross and out of the tomb to show us that love is the most powerful thing in the world, that God can't be defeated, and that God's truth cannot be killed. Easter changed a martyrdom into a triumph. It turned a disaster into a coronation. It turned a dark, ugly cross into a shining symbol of victory. Today, when we look at the cross with Easter eyes, we see some amazing, dependable, timeless lessons that will change our lives if we take them seriously and learn them well. Let's look together at a few of these.

The Cross Shows Us How to Love Unconditionally

Jesus' cross is *agape*—a symbol of God's uncalculated goodwill and love for all people, love in all circumstances, love with no strings attached, love that keeps no score of wrongs, love with no conditions. More than anything else, this is what Jesus came to teach us—how to love unconditionally.

In Jesus, we see what God is like. In Jesus, God is saying, "Look, this is how I love all of you. My love for you is unconditional. Nothing you can do will stop me from loving you. You can betray me, deny me, taunt me, beat me, curse me, spit on me, nail me to a cross . . . and I'm going to keep on loving you! There is nothing in the world that you can do to me that will stop me from loving you. I love you like that—unconditionally!"

And that is the way God wants us to love one another. You see, I can't say, "I will love you if you are good to me" or "I will love you if you are nice to me" or "I will love you if you love me back." I can't say that and live in the spirit of Christ. The only way I can live in his spirit is to love unconditionally, to love expecting nothing in return, to love unselfishly.

Let me ask you something. Do you love anybody like that? The cross reminds us that we are to love unconditionally.

The Cross Shows Us How to Suffer Creatively

Easter dramatically reminds us that defeats can be turned into victories.

Have you heard about the minister who stepped into his pulpit on Good Friday and preached a powerful sermon that was only five words long? He said, simply, "It's Friday . . . but Sunday's coming!"

Some years ago, Leslie Weatherhead put it like this: "The cross looked like defeat to the disciples. It felt like defeat to Jesus. It was called defeat by the world. But God made it God's greatest victory."

This is the message of Easter. God can turn defeats into victories. God can take the bad things this world can dish out and redeem them, and somehow make good come out of them. When something bad happens to us, we have to learn that the key question is not, "Why did this happen?" but rather, "Where does it lead?"

The cross shows us how to love unconditionally and how to suffer creatively.

The Cross Shows Us How to Live Sacrificially

Some years ago, there was a young professional baseball player who prided himself in being a great hitter. He knew he could make it big in the Major League if he could just get his chance. For several years he bounced around in the Minor Leagues. Finally one year, toward the end of the season, the Major League parent team brought him up to help them as they were in the thick of a heated pennant race. At last, his dream had come true—he was on a Major League team! But he was also a rookie, and promptly they put him on the bench.

Day after day went by, and the rookie was itching to bat. Finally one day, the manager called for the rookie to pinch hit for another batter. This was the dramatic moment he had dreamed of for so long—a crucial game, in the last inning, with the score tied and a runner on first base. This was his big moment, but he couldn't believe his eyes: The coaches were giving him the signal to "sacrifice"—in other words, to bunt, to make an out on purpose in order to advance the runner to second base, in the hope that the next hitter could bring him in for a run.

Well, the rookie ignored the signal, took three hefty swings, and struck out. When he returned to the dugout, he was met by a red-faced, angry manager who said, "Son, what's the matter with you? Didn't you see the signal to sacrifice?"

"Yes sir, I saw it," said the rookie, "but I didn't think you really meant it!"

Isn't that what we say to God? On page after page of the Scriptures, God says to us, "Sacrifice; sacrifice, love others, think of others, lay down your life for others, lose yourself for others, sacrifice yourself for the good of the team, be self-giving!" That's what God says to us, but we are not sure he really means it. Well, Jesus shows us that he meant it on the cross!

The cross shows us how to love unconditionally, how to suffer creatively, and how to live sacrificially.

The Cross Shows Us How to Celebrate Victoriously

The great minister W. E. Sangster in later years contracted an incurable neurological disease that caused progressive muscular atrophy. His muscles would gradually waste away, his voice would fail, and his throat would become unable to swallow. On Easter morning, just a few weeks before his death, he wrote to his daughter these touching words: "It's terrible to wake up on Easter morning and have no voice to shout, 'He is Risen!'—but it would be still more terrible to have a voice and not want to shout."

You and I have voices, and we have the good news of Easter. And because of that good news, with God's help, and by God's grace we can love unconditionally, we can suffer creatively, we can live sacrificially, and we can celebrate Easter victoriously every day of our lives.

Every day, if we listen closely, we can hear the triumphant voice of Mary Magdalene shouting, "He is risen! He is risen!"

DISCUSSION GUIDE

for
I Hear Voices, and That's a Good Thing!

BY JAMES W. MOORE

JOHN D. SCHROEDER

1. I Hear the Voice of Jesus Saying, "Let Your Light Shine"

Snapshot Summary

This chapter is about saints and reminds us that saints make it easy to believe in God, they believe the best in the worst of times, and they do extraordinary things in extraordinary ways.

Reflection / Discussion Questions

1. Share your interest in this book and what you hope to gain from the experience of reading and discussing it.
2. What thoughts or images come to mind when you hear the word *saint*?

3. Explain why the word *saint* is a "good word gone wrong."
4. Reflect on / discuss what saints do and say to make it easy for others to believe in God.
5. Describe some ways we can make goodness attractive and inspire faith.
6. Why do we all need to believe the best things in the worst times?
7. Describe ways in which saints are different from other people. Are saints perfect?
8. What does it mean to do ordinary things in extraordinary ways?
9. What makes it difficult to love the unlovable? How can this difficulty be overcome?
10. What additional thoughts or questions from this chapter would you like to explore?

Prayer: *Dear God, thank you for saints and for giving us the ability to let our light shine. Help us to help others believe, believe the best, and do extraordinary works in your name. Amen.*

2. I Hear the Voice of Abraham Saying, "Let There Be No Strife Between You and Me"

Snapshot Summary

This chapter explores the gracious spirit of Abraham and applies it to the world scene, to families, and to the way we think about God.

Reflection / Discussion Questions

1. Share an image from war that is etched into your heart and mind.

2. Name some of the causes of strife in the world today.
3. Reflect on / discuss the situation of strife faced by Abraham.
4. What does it mean to be a peacemaker?
5. Reflect on / discuss the gracious spirit of Abraham. How can that spirit be applied to the world scene?
6. How can we all be peacemakers?
7. Why do we hate? Reflect on / discuss the causes.
8. Reflect on / discuss some keys to resolving family squabbles.
9. How can God help us be peacemakers? What can we learn from the ministry of Jesus?
10. What additional thoughts or questions from this chapter would you like to explore?

Prayer: *Dear God, thank you for peacemakers and for the work they do in our world. Help us be peacemakers also and show your love to others. Amen.*

3. I Hear the Voice of Joseph Saying, "You Meant Evil Against Me, But God Meant It for Good"

Snapshot Summary

This chapter examines the four basic questions that are often raised when life goes wrong: Whose fault is it? How do we respond? How can this situation be redeemed? And where is God?

Reflection / Discussion Questions

1. Share a time when you came face-to-face with trouble.
2. Trouble comes in all shapes and sizes. Name some common troubles.

3. What troubles do you think are the worst and why?
4. Reflect on / discuss what happened to Joseph and the circumstances that brought about those events.
5. What do you admire about Joseph?
6. When things go wrong, why is fault-finding a first response? What is more important than finding fault?
7. Reflect on / discuss some of the many options we have in responding to trouble. Which options for responding to trouble do you believe are the worst or the best?
8. What should happen for a situation to be redeemed?
9. When we face trouble, where is God?
10. What additional thoughts or questions from this chapter would you like to explore?

Prayer: *Dear God, thank you for being with us in times of trouble. Remind us that solutions exist, and that we can turn to you and others for help. Amen.*

4. I Hear the Voice of Moses Saying, "Do Not Be Afraid . . . The Lord Will Fight for You . . . Go Forward"

Snapshot Summary

This chapter uses the story of Moses to teach us about seeing to believe, seeing to forgive, and seeing how to trust.

Reflection / Discussion Questions

1. Share a time when you found yourself facing the wrong direction.
2. Reflect on / discuss why the way in which we see things is so crucial.
3. Reflect on / discuss why different people often see the same situation differently.

4. What was the situation facing Moses? What did he see? How did he respond? What was the result?
5. What do you admire about Moses?
6. Reflect on / discuss what needs to happen before we can believe. Why is believing seeing?
7. What often prevents people from forgiving? Name some common obstacles.
8. How do we obtain a spirit of forgiveness?
9. Reflect on / discuss what it means to trust in God.
10. What additional thoughts or questions from this chapter would you like to explore?

Prayer: *Dear God, thank you for helping us go forward in life. Help us to believe, to trust, and to forgive during our journey. Amen.*

5. I Hear the Voice of King Saul Saying, "Remember to Put God First"

Snapshot Summary

This chapter looks at the dangers of success, including losing our priorities and our sense of purpose, resenting the successes of others, losing our family, and forgetting our dependence on God and others.

Reflection / Discussion Questions

1. Share a time when you found success to be dangerous.
2. Describe some of the dangers of success. Which dangers are the worst?
3. Is it easier to cope with hard times or with success? Share your thoughts on this.
4. Reflect on / discuss the tragic story of King Saul.

5. What causes us often to forget what is really important and what matters?
6. How and why do we lose our priorities and our sense of purpose?
7. Reflect on / discuss why we sometimes resent the success of others.
8. How can success negatively impact families?
9. Reflect on / discuss some signs that you are losing your sense of gratitude to God and others.
10. What additional thoughts or questions from this chapter would you like to explore?

Prayer: *Dear God, thank you for putting us first. Help us always put you first and not allow success to damage our relationships. Amen.*

6. I Hear the Voice of Esther Saying, "Don't Miss Your Moment"

Snapshot Summary

This chapter focuses on missed moments: how we see the "missed-moment syndrome" in Scriptures, how Esther seized her moment, and how Esther used the courage she possessed.

Reflection / Discussion Questions

1. Share a time when you *experienced* your moment.
2. Now share a time when you *missed* your moment.
3. Reflect on / discuss some of the examples of the missed-moment syndrome as found in the Scriptures.
4. What lessons can we learn from the story of Esther?
5. What do you admire most about Esther?
6. Reflect on / discuss how and why courage is an essential element of seizing the moment.

7. Name some causes that lead to missed moments.
8. Reflect on / discuss the lasting damage caused by missed moments.
9. How can we prevent missing our moment? How can God help?
10. What additional thoughts or questions from this chapter would you like to explore?

Prayer: *Dear God, thank you for each and every moment of life you give us. Help us live life to the fullest, never missing a moment, and help us to help others along the way. Amen.*

7. I Hear the Voice of Daniel Saying, "Read the Handwriting on the Wall and Tell It Like It Is"

Snapshot Summary

This chapter examines how we see and miss the handwriting on the wall because of lack of understanding, being disillusioned, and lacking courage to "tell it like it is."

Reflection / Discussion Questions

1. Share a time when you saw the handwriting on the wall.
2. Why do people have trouble telling it like it is?
3. What lessons can we learn from the story of Daniel and Belshazzar?
4. What impresses you most about Daniel?
5. How and why do people become preoccupied?
6. What can people miss because they are preoccupied?
7. Reflect on / discuss the dangers of not being familiar with the Bible and not reading it daily.
8. What can happen when people become disillusioned?

9. Why does it take courage to "tell it like it is"?
10. What additional thoughts or questions from this chapter would you like to explore?

Prayer: *Dear God, thank you for the lessons we can learn from Daniel. Help us have courage to tell it like it is and give us the ability to read the handwriting on the wall. Amen.*

8. I Hear the Voice of Micah Saying, "Do Justice, Love Kindness, and Walk Humbly With Your God"

Snapshot Summary

This chapter looks to the words of Micah in an exploration of the state of our morals as a country. It shows how we are in danger of losing touch with goodness, becoming a society of splinter groups, and thinking that freedom of religion means freedom from religion.

Reflection / Discussion Questions

1. Explain what it means to be demoralized.
2. Share a time when you experienced or witnessed an act of demoralization.
3. Do you think the United States is suffering from demoralization? Describe your reasoning.
4. What are some signs or symptoms of demoralization?
5. Reflect on / discuss the possible consequences of moral drifting.
6. Why are Americans in danger of losing touch with goodness?
7. What's the cause of splinter groups and special interests? What dangers do they pose?

8. Reflect on / discuss attacks on religion in the news and other media. What are the negative effects?
9. Reflect on / discuss what you believe we need to do to survive and recover. What signs of hope do you see?
10. What additional thoughts or questions from this chapter would you like to explore?

Prayer: *Dear God, we thank you for our country and for all you have given us and this nation. Help us do justice, love kindness, and walk humbly with you. Amen.*

9. I Hear the Voice of Mary Saying, "Let It Be to Me According to Your Word"

Snapshot Summary

This chapter looks at the good news of Christmas through the words and actions of Mary. It explores the faith of Mary, the encouragement of Elizabeth, and the gracious, loving, saving action of God.

Reflection / Discussion Questions

1. Share a favorite childhood Christmas memory.
2. Reflect on / discuss what Christmas can teach us about life.
3. Reflect on / discuss the story of Mary and her faith. What can we learn from her?
4. What do you admire about Mary?
5. How did Mary respond to the message from the angel? Why was her response remarkable?
6. Reflect on / discuss the difficulties Mary experienced.

7. How did Elizabeth respond to Mary's news? Who in your life has given the kind of support to you that Elizabeth gave Mary?
8. Reflect on / discuss the power of love, encouragement, and affirmation as shown through Mary.
9. Name some of the ways we see and experience the saving action of God today.
10. What additional thoughts or questions from this chapter would you like to explore?

Prayer: *Dear God, thank you for the gift of Christmas and all it means to us. Help us remember the importance of faith, encouragement, and your loving, saving actions that sustain us. Amen.*

Chapter 10. I Hear the Voice of Jesus Saying, "Love One Another as I Have Loved You"

Snapshot Summary

This chapter shows us how the power of love can heal us physically, emotionally, and spiritually.

Reflection / Discussion Questions

1. Share a time when you experienced the healing power of love.
2. What does it mean to have a warm and compassionate Christian spirit?
3. Discuss how and why love can heal us physically.
4. What role did love play in the healing power of Jesus during his ministry?
5. List people who need love today.
6. Name some ways we can share the love of Jesus with those in need of healing and support.

7. Reflect on / discuss the power love has to heal people emotionally.
8. Name some emotional conditions that respond to love, understanding, and encouragement.
9. Love has the power to heal us spiritually. How do we obtain spiritual healing?
10. What additional thoughts or questions from this chapter would you like to explore?

Prayer: *Dear God, thank you for the healing power of love that changes lives. Help us use the power of love to help others heal physically, emotionally, and spiritually. Amen.*

11. I Hear the Voice of Paul Saying, "The Greatest of These Is Love"

Snapshot Summary

This chapter looks to the words of the apostle Paul in seeking to teach our children to be loving persons by modeling respect and sacrifice, and by showing them Christ's example.

Reflection / Discussion Questions

1. Share a time when you missed the message or had a misunderstanding.
2. Reflect on / discuss the problems of the Corinthian church and the causes of these problems.
3. How did Paul respond to and attempt to resolve the problems at Corinth?
4. Reflect on / discuss what Paul says about love in 1 Corinthians 13.
5. Reread 1 Corinthians 13. What phrase in this "Love Chapter" inspires you the most? Explain why.

6. Reflect on / discuss why love is the key, the secret, and the answer.
7. How can we teach children to be loving through the example of respect?
8. Give some examples of personal sacrifice that can help children be more loving.
9. Reflect on / discuss ways to help children accept the living Christ in their lives.
10. What additional thoughts or questions from this chapter would you like to explore?

Prayer: *Dear God, thank you for reminding us that love is the key and the answer. Help us love others just as you love us. Amen.*

12. I Hear the Voice of Mary Magdalene Saying, "He Is Risen"

Snapshot Summary

This chapter uses the story of Mary Magdalene to explore the significance of the cross of Christ, showing us how to love unconditionally, suffer creatively, live sacrificially, and celebrate victoriously.

Reflection / Discussion Questions

1. Share a time when you experienced a surprise or a surprise ending.
2. Discuss the journey of Mary Magdalene to the tomb, and her discovery. Describe the feelings and emotions you believe she would have been experiencing.
3. As the author describes them, what three things did the cross represent in the time of Jesus? What does the cross represent today?

4. In what ways does the cross show us how to love unconditionally?
5. Share a time when you experienced unconditional love.
6. Reflect on / discuss creative suffering and give an example of it.
7. Describe some ways we can live sacrificially.
8. How can we celebrate Easter victoriously every day of our lives?
9. What additional thoughts or questions from this chapter would you like to explore?
10. How has your reading, reflection, and/or discussion of this book helped you?

Prayer: *Dear God, thank you for this small-group experience and for the members of this group. Thank you for their contributions and support. Bless all of us as we go our separate ways, and help us always hear those positive voices from the Bible that seek to guide us along your path. Amen.*